The Future Makers:
A Journey to People who are Changing the World –
and What we can Learn from Them

Joanna Hafenmayer Stefańska and Wolfgang Hafenmayer

THE FUTURE
makers

A Journey to People who are Changing the World – and what we can learn from them

Greenleaf
PUBLISHING

© 2013 Greenleaf Publishing Limited

Published by Greenleaf Publishing Limited
Aizlewood's Mill
Nursery Street
Sheffield S3 8GG
UK
www.greenleaf-publishing.com

First published (in German) by oekom verlag, Munich, 2007
Translated from German by David Hünlich and Jessica Plummer

Printed in the UK on environmentally friendly, acid-free paper
from managed forests by CPI Group (UK) Ltd, Croydon

British Library Cataloguing in Publication Data:
   A catalogue record for this book is available from the British Library.

ISBN-13: 978-1-906093-85-3 [paperback]
ISBN-13: 978-1-907643-58-3 [hardback]
ISBN-13: 978-1-907643-59-0 [electronic]

Contents

Preface

With this book, we would like to take you on a journey. On this journey you will meet a number of special people who simultaneously pursue successful, professional careers while making the world a better place in which to live. They do not compromise on either of these aims. They are people who find innovative and sustainable solutions to the immense challenges we all face, both now and in the future. Subsequently, we call them the 'Future Makers'.

We met these people during our expedition around the world a few years ago and, at the time, they seemed to be a rare species. But increasingly we now meet people like them every day, both at home and in many countries and cities around the world. It seems that Future Makers are everywhere and that they will be the ones shaping and changing the world's economy and society in the years to come. We wonder, are you a Future Maker?

The two of us – both 30 years of age and successful in our careers – left our previous jobs behind for one year in order to get to know different personalities from around the globe. We met many more innovators than we had ever dared hope for. Returning from our year-long tour, we had encountered over 230 interview partners on all continents, including businesspeople, computer experts, engineers, dancers, art historians, human rights activists and doctors. Despite all having aspirations of being professionally successful, these innovators were also highly committed to supporting beneficial causes, creating a positive impact on society and truly enjoying what they do – they are genuine Future Makers.

In Part II of this book we provide an extensive introduction into the lives of 23 of the 235 Future Makers we interviewed. The encounters we experienced during our trip changed us. While over time some of the people portrayed here have further developed their organisations or moved on to new challenges, we are quite sure that they will inspire and motivate you as they have us – especially if you sometimes wonder what your job offers beyond the money and career you make and ask yourself for what purpose you want to invest your precious time, talents and energy. You will find even more inspiring profiles on the inspirational platform, www.thefuturemakers.net.

The end of this book, Part III, presents you with a guide that makes concrete proposals for your future and aims to support you as you question your professional career more thoroughly, examine it critically and embark on your own personal journey. We want to encourage you to reflect on your existence and show you how you can make your vision become a reality. The encouraging examples provided by the Future Makers are thought-provoking when it comes to developing and redirecting your career towards a happier life and personal contentment. Beyond this guide, you will find more helpful tools and services on www.myimpact.net. We wholeheartedly hope that this book inspires you to become a Future Maker too!

Joanna Hafenmayer Stefańska and Wolfgang Hafenmayer,
Zurich, autumn 2012

I

A WORLD TOUR WITH CONSEQUENCES

How the adventure of a world tour was born

It all began in the summer of 2004 when we made the decision to leave our home in Switzerland to embark on a tour around the world. For 12 months, we wanted to leave behind everything that had governed our lives up to then: family and friends, demanding jobs, our apartment and cars. Having had successful careers in the business sector, we wanted to take a step forward. In contrast to what we typically experienced in our own surroundings, we wanted to get to know people who pursued totally different aims in life and who made a positive impact on their fellow human beings through their professional dedication.

Many of our friends responded with surprise when they heard of our decision: 'What are you thinking? How did you get that idea?' they asked. It wasn't always easy to give plausible reasons for our motives: why we were not only planning to travel, but also to work. Why we were seeking to meet people who were committing themselves to social justice, ecological solutions and a sustainable quality of life in countries far away.

The reactions of our colleagues ranged from jealousy of the free and self-determined year ahead of us, to complete incomprehension. They wondered how we could jeopardise everything at such an important point in our careers, risking everything we had worked hard for, with the chance of losing it altogether. Most of our peers knew us as diligent, hard-working individuals with a lot of ambition. Of all the people they knew, they wondered how we could question our lifestyle.

Marketing for Bill Gates

We did not consider that our step was spectacular, let alone risky. In our excitement, we did not feel that we had a lot to lose. We were lucky to have grown up in a place and society with many opportunities, with great family backup and all the support we needed to take chances in life. We had both studied at and graduated from the University of St Gallen, which is one of the best universities in Europe. Wolfgang's field was business administration with a specialisation in information management and Joanna had studied political sciences with an emphasis on international relations. Since we had always completed our internships and worked while studying, it was easy for us to find challenging, well-paid jobs. In 2000, Joanna started as the second employee of a telecommunications company. Thanks to the boom in innovative technologies, and with the help of American investors, the company expanded to 100 employees within a year. Of course, there were many exciting and challenging moments. The big lesson, however, came when the investors ran out of money and simultaneously decided to cancel their activities in over ten countries. Unfortunately, Switzerland was one of the countries affected. Since the stock market had suffered a recent downturn in the spring of 2001, no alternative investors could be found within the required short time span.

As a consequence, Joanna found herself working for a final three-month period, during which the company was liquidated and the employees were laid off. Even though this was an invaluable lesson with regard to good management abilities in times of crisis, it was an unforgiving time. Coming from this situation, it was pleasant for her to find an entrepreneurial, results-oriented and stable environment at Microsoft. In the following years things progressed well for Joanna. Hired as a marketing assistant, she was promoted to product manager for one of the company's most important products at the age of 28. Soon she had the chance to establish Microsoft's information technology (IT) security initiative, which had been declared to be strategically important, in Switzerland.

In addition to intensive, long working days, dealing with the newest technical equipment and attending yearly meetings with thousands of co-workers in the USA, a number of fascinating events went along with the job too. With unbelievable speed, a string of events unravelled and hardly left any time for reflection. After another 18 months of high-speed work and managing two jobs at the same time, she received a number of awards in the name of Bill Gates's company. It was at that moment, while everything was going perfectly, Joanna told her colleagues that she would be going on a trip around the world. She wanted to talk to people who dedicated their lives to social and ecological causes.

Plane–office–hotel–office–plane

At the same time, Wolfgang had to conquer 80-hour weeks during his consultancy training at Bain & Company, one of the most successful strategy consulting firms worldwide. Having a job at the Swiss office meant that Wolfgang had to take an aeroplane to Zurich every weekend and then catch another every Monday morning in order to travel elsewhere. During the week he had to convince customers across Europe that lack of experience could be compensated for easily by increased dedication and faster learning. It was not uncommon for Wolfgang to catch only a glimpse of the cities he travelled to on his way from the airport to the customer's office and then back to the hotel. Actually, it was not even important whether he was working in Budapest, Milan or London. The learning curve was very steep and the international teams he worked with exposed him to high expectations on a daily basis.

After his intense and demanding apprenticeship at Bain & Company, Wolfgang joined a small team of experienced management consultants and IT specialists who had just founded the consulting firm Consileon. Because the next big customer was already waiting for a consultant, Wolfgang only had one night free after changing jobs to his new employer; the next morning he continued in the same vein, only this time with a new business card and a new customer. However, he now had more responsibility and a real opportunity to help shape the enterprise.

Having advanced to the position of executive director in the Swiss office at the age of 29, it was Wolfgang's primary task to attend to new and rather difficult customers. In spite of the difficult market situation, Consileon successfully grew from seven to 70 employees within three years. At every company Christmas party the management was able to herald new record figures. This was a remarkable development for such a young enterprise. The expansion was likely the result of an unusually frugal company philosophy and culture, combined with the passion and hard work of experienced professionals – a trait the founding partners had acquired through their own experiences. In the past, they had seen how greed and high-handedness led to the demise of other companies and how catastrophic the effects were for the families of the employees. But Consileon was far removed from this as the company moved from success to success.

Wolfgang's work made him very happy and offered him exactly the degree of daily challenges he had wished for during his studies. How could he possibly think about leaving for a world trip with things the way they were?

Is something missing here?

According to the prevailing criteria of success, everything seemed to be running perfectly well: we had well-paid, challenging and fun jobs. Our careers were coming along swimmingly and for our age we already had more responsibility than prior generations would have had as 50-year-old senior executives. Materially, we were already able to afford more than was necessary to lead a carefree life. Eventually, however, we both also had the feeling that this could not be everything. We were both quite sure that, were we to look back at the end of our lives, we would not be happy with ourselves if we simply continued in this way. Something important seemed to be missing, but we couldn't find it in the way we were living our daily lives.

When we looked around at our environment, we were not the only ones who were experiencing this. Even though many of our colleagues had attained responsibility in interesting, often well-paid jobs and were sincerely committed to this responsibility, we did not always have the feeling that all of them were really happy. The phrase, 'at the moment things are a bit stressful' became a slogan. Dissatisfaction with professional life was often silenced by 'retail therapy', a rise in salary or, at the most, by switching jobs to work for a competitor. It was not that our colleagues were affected by tragedy or had not found a suitable partner in life. On the contrary – some got married, made plans to have children and were in good health. Nevertheless, people often voiced complaints and recurring grievances. Again and again they expressed hope that everything would 'get better soon'.

We started asking ourselves how everything *could* get better soon if everyone remained occupied with the same things. Weren't we almost forced to continue with our jobs because of our new, ever more costly hobbies? Didn't we permanently have to work and earn more money simply because of fixed costs? Weren't people taking more and more responsibility without taking the time to discover and reflect on their true needs?

The trip begins in your mind

These thoughts occupied our minds constantly. We started reading and asking ourselves many questions: What exactly was it that bothered us about our current life? The common suggestion of aiming to achieve a 'work-life balance' was not a true solution. Rather, our dissatisfaction had a deeper reason. We were quite sure that it had something to do with the meaning of our work in itself, the sense we made of it and the feeling that work could potentially offer us much more. Then we started to ponder our future by asking fundamental questions: What do we want to look back on one day? What do we want our friends and family to say about us at the end of our lives? Should it be something like: 'They toiled for hours every day at the office to live an affluent lifestyle?' And, if our current jobs were not giving us a feeling of purpose and fulfilment, what were the alternatives? How far away from our professional territory would we have to look in order to find a job that brought us satisfaction?

While searching, we quickly discovered many interesting contemporary questions about the responsibility of companies. We came across the terms 'corporate social responsibility' and 'corporate citizenship'. We also encountered a number of ethical and ecological topics such as the ecological responsibilities of policy, economy and society, sustainable development, clean technology, social entrepreneurship and philanthropy. This appealed to us and we felt attracted to it: something seemed to be hidden here that could lead us onto the right path.

During this stage of reflection and exploration, we also visited a business conference co-organised by Microsoft under the motto 'Realising Potential'. During a discussion panel of leading economists, a director of the International Red Cross was confronted with a statement that things must be relatively easy for her, since the success of her organisation was not measured by its financial returns and nor was she forced to produce revenue. Doris Pfister, whom we later got to know in personal conversation, answered very calmly:

While we are not being judged by profits, we are being very strictly evaluated by the impact we have on the lives of other people. We have to show how many children we vaccinate, how many prisoners we visit and how many people we help during catastrophes.

Impact over profit

It often happens in life that you hear something and, as what you heard combines with all of the other things that are on your mind, your own thoughts begin to take shape. In this case it immediately became clear to us: life is not about profit, but rather, it is about impact!

We understand impact as our contribution to – or the effects of our actions on – our environment and society. Are other people better off because we exist, are we contributing something good *or* are we actually destroying things? Accordingly, every individual's impact can be positive or negative. In Part III of this book we will explain in more detail when impact is positive or negative for us.

As consultants, we were used to establishing hypotheses about how something could become better and underpin these with hard facts. So, the as yet incomplete hypothesis that suggested itself read: 'You will be happy and content in life, if you help others through your activities, if you have a positive impact on the life of your fellow human beings.' Suddenly, this thought seemed to express, in a simple and clear way, exactly what we had been looking for. Our conclusion was that we wanted to get to know such people. To be precise, we wanted to meet people who contributed positively to their environment through their jobs.

From our readings we realised that we needed to travel further than the banks of Lake Zurich, where we had been living for the last few years, to find such people. We would have to travel the world, to countries and continents far away. But how and where would we find all these people, and who would want to talk to us in first place?

The appeal of the will – and of social entrepreneurs

During the next few weeks we were granted an experience for the first time that several of our future interviewees would later confirm: if you really want something with all your heart and make an effort to get it, opportunities will open up that you had never thought possible. It turned out that one of Wolfgang's best friends from Bain & Company was working for the Schwab Foundation for Social Entrepreneurship[1] in Geneva for a year. He was organising a meeting in Campinas, Brazil, with all the social entrepreneurs who had so far been accepted to Schwab's worldwide network. We had previously read a lot about social entrepreneurs, people who innovatively, pragmatically and sustainably dedicated their entrepreneurial means towards ground-breaking social change. We certainly did not want to miss the chance to get to know several of them and to discuss our project idea with them!

So, in the autumn of 2004, Wolfgang celebrated his birthday in Campinas. After a fantastic week and many unique encounters, our decision was made: we would travel around the world to visit people who make a positive impact on society. It would be an exciting, informative and unparalleled experience. Even though we did not know what 'positive impact' looked like when put into practice, we both knew that if we were to find out, this trip could not be avoided. Though we had to finance the trip with our own means, the prospect of the encounters and insights that awaited us made it more than worthwhile.

Circling the globe with a cause

It is hard to believe how fast things can go. Only five months after our trip to Brazil, we had left our jobs, terminated our lease, sold our cars and stored away our belongings in our parents' basements. We founded the enterprise MyImpact and launched the web platform www.myimpact.net, where we wanted to report directly on our meetings. In April 2005 we were on our way. Equipped with a 'round the world' ticket of 20 flights (sadly this meant we would be generating CO_2, but our partnership with CO2OL, an agency for corporate climate protection, would help to counterbalance the effects) a backpack each packed with all we needed to cover our needs for a year, our laptops, a recording device and cameras. In advance, we had established at least one contact for an interview in each country we aimed to visit. Since we did not wish to hold more than 30 conversations, this part of our trip seemed manageable.

One year, five continents and 26 countries later, we were, however, over-whelmed: not only by the new impressions which we had tried to capture in 14,000 pictures, but most of all by the 235 encounters we had with incredible people. In our eyes, these people really deserved to be called role models and Future Makers. So in the end, the 30 conversations we had planned to

---

1   The Schwab Foundation for Social Entrepreneurship – initiated by Klaus Schwab, founder of the World Economic Forum, awards the 'Social Entrepreneur of the Year'. A hybrid between Bill Gates and Mother Teresa is sought: someone who can implement innovative solutions to social and ecological questions in a business framework.

hold became 235 interviews. We would not have missed a single one of them. Moreover, we will never forget any of them.

The more conversations we had, and the further we delved into our research, the more interesting people to whom we were introduced became. Meeting these fascinating personalities almost became addicting. Our learning curve with regard to solutions to social and ecological challenges virtually exploded – which was also supported by applicable literature that we devoured on our way and later sent home in packages. We found our interviewees through various channels such as networks,[2] publications, research and personal recommendations. From the very beginning, we deliberately avoided evaluating people by the size or importance of the positive impact they made on society as comparison would not do justice to anyone. We simply wanted to find stories that would touch and inspire people who are interested in trendsetting solutions.

What did the trip change? What is different today?

'The real voyage of discovery consists not in seeking new landscapes but in having new eyes.' *Marcel Proust*

Nothing can describe our world trip and our experiences better than this statement by Marcel Proust. After several years working in Europe, we wanted to meet people who were not only interested in their own career and their personal environment, but who also considered solving worldwide social challenges to be part of their responsibility. What we experienced led us to view the world with new eyes and we realised that things cannot be judged easily as they are much more complicated than we imagined. We have become more aware of the quality of life our surroundings offer and we value it highly. We made some changes to our lifestyle and consumption and we continue to travel often in order not to lose sight of realities in the rest of the world.

Most of all, however, we also want to contribute with our own energy and work to sustainably improve the well-being of people. Since we continue to work intensively, we can exert the greatest influence through our occupations. In order to continue creating an overall contribution towards a positive impact on the world, we want not only to be mindful of our experience, abilities and interests – but also our own needs, such as family and health.

---

2 We would like to thank Ashoka, Avina, the Schwab Foundation, the Skoll Foundation, the World Business Council for Sustainable Development, Echoing Green, WISE and LEVAL among others.

Our positive impact through meeting new challenges

'Happiness is when what you think, what you say, and what you do are in harmony.' **Mahatma Gandhi**

We went on our world trip without having any concrete plans for what would happen after that. We didn't know how the trip would change us and what effect it would have on our future. We were, however, ready to accept the various professional challenges we discovered and also to give up our material standard of living to be able to maintain a positive impact professionally. However, just as we landed in Zurich, a year full of exciting challenges waited for us.

During our final interviews at an oikos conference,[3] we got to know Antoinette Hunziker-Ebneter, who was starting a new asset management company after years of working in the higher echelons of management in financial businesses and the stock exchange. Our experiences turned out to be extremely relevant for her aim of focusing exclusively on sustainable investments. Just a few weeks later, we were developing the concept for a new type of asset-management company called Forma Futura[4] with her team of experienced bankers. Among other advancements, we developed an innovative business model and a sustainable-assets assessment system.

At the same time in June 2006, Wolfgang started his job as an investment manager at BonVenture,[5] the first social venture fund in German-speaking countries. BonVenture supports organisations and enterprises that work for ecological or social business causes through financial means, consulting and a network of experts. Owing to the partially misguided framework of today's economic system, the planned financial revenue of those supported by Bon-Venture is not high enough to be considered a relevant investment for traditional venture capital businesses. By the same token, the initial phase bears risks that are too high for banks. In situations like this, the sector of social venture capital or 'venture philanthropy', which grew during the 1990s in the USA and gained traction in Europe around the year 2000, offers an adequate approach that fosters exactly those innovative solutions. Wolfgang's work with BonVenture was both outstanding and fascinating due to its positive impact on the environment and the innovative power of the investment management companies.

However, in the autumn of 2007 an opportunity arose to build a global-venture philanthropy team for the Princely Family of Liechtenstein and use this as a platform to help many others become involved with professional

---

3 oikos is the international student organisation for sustainable economics and management and a leading reference point for the promotion of sustainability change agents. www.oikos-international.org

4 www.formafutura.com/en/index.php

5 www.bonventure.de/en/home.html

philanthropy and impact investing. The opportunity of leveraging tremendous resources to create a positive societal impact was too tempting for Wolfgang to stay with BonVenture. He therefore took on the challenge of building LGT Venture Philanthropy,[6] with the aim of improving the quality of life for less-advantaged people. To achieve this mission, Wolfgang hired a team of more than 20 outstanding impact-investing professionals based in six continents, within the first five years. All of them select and support organisations with outstanding social and environmental impact. With tailored financing, management know-how[7] and relevant networks, LGT Venture Philanthropy helps these organisations grow and scale their influence. Until 2012 its portfolio organisations have improved the lives of over 7 million less-advantaged people worldwide. Based on the knowledge generated through its investing activities around the world, LGT Venture Philanthropy advises clients how to start or improve their own philanthropic impact-investing engagement and inspires people by sharing their stories of great solutions to global challenges.[8,9] Today, its broad range of clients benefit from the team, experience, systems, processes and networks that were built to realise the philanthropic impact-investing engagement for the Princely Family of Liechtenstein and LGT Venture Philanthropy. After this five-year fascinating journey, Wolfgang is now more than ever convinced that the potential to create positive solutions is tremendous. Based on what was built, he is, together with many other people who are motivated to create a positive environmental impact, looking forward to creating a 'smiling world'.

After the basis for Forma Futura was set, Joanna was convinced that large, international corporations would play a crucial role in the future development of a global society. She joined Microsoft's Swiss executive team in the newly created position of organisation, innovation and sustainability officer. Because of her earlier work with the company, she knew the challenges faced by the core business and went on to develop an environmental-sustainability strategy for Switzerland and contributed to the establishment of the first global environmental board. Through her focus on creating win-win situations for business and society, she was able to implement a number of innovative initiatives such as the National Home Office Day, which was later replicated by several countries around the world. As rewarding as the work was, the need to convince colleagues that a different focus to support the initiatives and see them as valuable contributions – and not merely nice-to-have, sideline activities – was also required.

In the most difficult times, as often happens, a new opportunity came up. The US-based Aspen Institute launched a fellowship programme for professionals in the private sector to create innovations at the intersection of

6 www.lgtvp.com
7 www.lgtvp.com/icats
8 www.lgtvp.com/HOPS/Smiling-World-Initiative-(1).aspx
9 www.lgtvp.com/HOPS.aspx

business and social value. The name, the First Movers,[10] was well chosen. In the class of 2010, Joanna met a number of amazing, inspiring and ambitious professionals who were working in many countries and companies around the world, and who possessed a smartness and tenacity that was just as mind-blowing as the encounters we made during our global journey. They were social intrapreneurs, a rare but strongly developing species. Inspired by this experience, and with great and appreciated support from Microsoft, Joanna started focusing on social intrapreneurship and responsible leadership, brought together a group of companies which focused on developing their leaders in a responsible way and finally left Microsoft to continue working exclusively on that topic.

This is where the spirits of the old and the new MyImpact converge and build on each other. Joanna relaunched www.myimpact.net and started a number of new services, such as seminars, workshops and coaching – all aiming in the same direction: to enable more people to have meaningful careers.

www.myimpact.net gives an overview of those services and provides helpful tools for the journey to a meaningful career. The newly launched platform, www.thefuturemakers.net is a collection of inspiring stories of Future Makers – those from this book and beyond.

Now, let us again focus on the life stories of the 23 fascinating men and women that we chose out of the 235 interviews we conducted around the world for this book. They show that your impact does not depend on how old or young, how rich or poor, or how successful or gifted you are.

Evolving your professional life in a new direction certainly requires courage and a certain willingness to take a risk. It is challenging and not easy to give up comfortable habits to rearrange your life. Excuses will show up quickly and insurmountable obstacles will make a new beginning seem impossible. Also, you will wander unknown roads that only few people have travelled before – there is little guidance and no standard procedure. Nevertheless, it is worthwhile to question the obstacles and test their real substance. Just like our interview partners did.

We have therefore arranged their stories by chapters according to the most common supposed hurdles and excuses:

- Chapter 1. 'I don't have the right professional background'

- Chapter 2. 'I'm too young or too old'

- Chapter 3. 'I am not financially secure'

- Chapter 4. 'I am already successful with what I'm doing'

- Chapter 5. 'What will others think of me?'

---

10 www.aspeninstitute.org/policy-work/business-society/First-Movers-Fellowship-Program/2010-first-movers

The end of each chapter features a piece of insight: if you want to make a positive contribution towards a better life on earth, there are always means and ways to reach it. What is beautiful and encouraging is that you become a new person on your journey of impact.

When your professional life is permeated by a feeling of purpose and meaning, you will see that your own commitment has the positive outcome you hoped for. Let yourself be inspired by our trip through a world full of solutions – created by role models who deserve to be called Future Makers for the next centuries.

II

THE PORTRAITS

1

'I don't have the right professional background'

What skills are required for engaging professionally in creating a more liveable world? Are special qualifications or a particular ability necessary for creating positive change?

The following stories show that every person is already perfectly equipped with their own skills, talents and experiences. Almost every professional background can be used to make the world better and more sustainable. You don't have to be a doctor, environmental scientist or social worker to have a meaningful life and job.

A good example of this is the former Londoner, Safia Minney. She originally came from a glamorous world of high-gloss magazines and advertisements. Today she sells sensible, but beautiful fashion in the framework of a fair-trade corporation, using the skills she gained in her original field.

Chris Eyre is another example. Chris was one of the very first successful Silicon Valley venture capitalists. After a decisive turning point in his life, he put his talent for making and increasing money, as well as his valuable financial network, into the service of charitable organisations.

Jim Fruchterman, an award-winning social entrepreneur, is a technology enthusiast through and through. But instead of using his pattern recognition expertise for the control systems of the American army's missile network, he went on to develop the first reading machine for the blind. Today he is the director of Benetech, a technology corporation which uses his innovations to create technologies for humanitarian uses. Jim says:

> Many first-class technology specialists who enter into contracts with us say: 'Fantastic! I have the skills to really help society'. They find thinking about meaningful solutions for other people and realising them with our help really wonderful. It's a lot of fun for all of us. And

I would rather tell my children that I do something good for the blind and disadvantaged than how many people have been killed by the missiles I constructed.

'Whenever a family gets money with the help of a junk-job and can buy fresh bread or send the kids to school, it is a wonderful feeling for me.'

Albina Ruiz Ríos
Child of the jungle, engineer,
specialist in waste disposal
systems, refuse queen
Lima, Peru

Albina Ruiz Ríos – From jungle girl to refuse queen

Albina Ruiz Ríos grew up in the San Martin region of Peru. Her childhood was spent somewhere beyond ancient Inca sites, between the wild rivers and gigantic trees of the Amazonian jungle. The nearest large city was Moyobamba or 'Big River' in English. Albina spent a lot of time dwelling here, the area was abundant in flora and fauna, surrounded by colourful plants and an animal kingdom so rich in species we can hardly imagine it. Her parents were farmers and owned a coffee plantation. They lived in harmony with nature because their livelihood literally depended on it. Albina was incredibly fortunate in that she was able to attend a Catholic covenant school. In this region of the world, being able to receive an education is a rare opportunity. The nuns taught her much more than the three Rs – she also learned about the value of education and the responsibility the educated have to others.

The refuse just bothers me!

'I always had the opinion that it was necessary to find new solutions. That is why I wanted to become an engineer.' Albina remembered when we met her. 'Since there was no university in my area, my father suggested that I go to Lima. He always supported me.'

So, when Albina was 18, she moved to Lima, the faraway capital, in order to commence her studies. During our interview, she recalled her first impressions of the bustling capital with a shudder: 'It was so different there!' She was the only woman in her field of study and felt disgusted by the huge, noisy city. Her brother, who had been living in Lima for several years, told her which thugs in the neighbourhood to avoid and how best to navigate traffic. Before she took her first bus trip – in the jungle she had always walked – she spent a few days at her brother's house. She lived with his family in a room in El Augustino, one of the many slums in which stranded immigrants live wall-to-wall with criminals. During her first days in the city, Albina hardly left her house. Apart from the deafening noise on the street, she was bothered by the gross, stinking refuse heaps that piled up everywhere in the slums, harming the environment and affecting people's health. Comparing this to the beauty of the jungle, she was appalled by what her eyes had to see and what her nose had to smell every day. 'How could the people in Lima ever be able to live with dignity when they were exposed to such filth and noxious odours every day?', she would ask herself as she removed the refuse whenever she could.

Seeing potential within her own profession

One day, Albina asked herself why she was studying engineering. After all, engineering is a job concerned with finding solutions. After a preparation year, which she passed with flying colours, she began her actual studies. In the meantime, she had somewhat settled into her new environment and the omnipresent rubbish heaps gave the emerging scientist the idea that she could use the abilities she learned for something other than the construction of new machines or tools. So, in the early 1990s, Albina started to look into the subject of waste from a scientist's point of view. She wanted to understand the problem as a system and hoped to solve it. She founded a student-workgroup, calculated the health expenses of families living in the slums, and spent days on days in libraries. She spent even more days in the refuse collection trucks of the well-to-do boroughs of Lima. By doing this, she began to understand the system by asking such questions as: How much refuse fits into one collection truck? Which routes are the most efficient? How is waste optimally separated in order to be recycled? Who should sort out what at what level? How do you make sure that the 'recycladores', those living off the refuse every day, don't lose all their income over night? Perhaps they can be offered permanent jobs? Who collects the fees, at what time and how?

Albina described the critical times she passed through when we visited her at the main office of 'Cuidad Saludable' (Clean City) in Lima. 'Waste is a problem and I lived amid the problem. I had written a thesis on an innovative waste disposal system for the slums and decided to implement it first in Lima, my new home town.' Albina's voice conveyed urgency and electrified the listener. She was smiling or laughing almost all the time. At the same time, her face had a look of determination and certainty.

Being a mother – and other careers

Albina wrote her doctoral thesis on the social and ecological implications of refuse utilisation. Her findings drew the attention of the mayor of Lima who consequently offered her a job, in which she was asked to implement her system in a pilot project. A hectic time followed, especially since Albina was only 21 and had recently married and given birth to a daughter. It was hard to find a balance in life. However, with the help of another student, it somehow worked out:

> Many were surprised that – being the best student of my age group – I wasn't working for a company and making good money. I just always wanted to improve the quality of other people's lives. Helping other people has always been more important to me than money or a career. I always lived in poor areas and in poor areas it is dirty. In order to make life as bearable as possible, people try

to help one another and are often innovative in the way in which they do it.

Satisfied with the first success of her waste disposal system, Albina deepened her knowledge by pursuing a master's degree in ecology and environmental management. Finally, she graduated after further studies in Basel, Switzerland. Parallel to this, she expanded her system to other boroughs of Lima.

A sophisticated system with many employment possibilities

The basic idea of her system is easy: the inhabitants of the slums usually spend up to US$10 a month on fighting diarrhoea and other hygiene-related illnesses, however, by investing this amount into a functioning waste collection service they consequently avoid a good portion of these illnesses. Simultaneously, Albina's system provides opportunities and income for a number of small-scale enterprises which have sprung up around the waste collection and recycling services. So, while some people pick up the refuse and collect the fees, others separate the waste and recycle a good part of it into new products – which generates a number of jobs. Often these jobs go to women who establish themselves an additional income, for example by composting part of the refuse and later selling it as fertiliser.

Albina manages to turn a chain of resource withdrawal into a chain of resource recovery – thereby creating jobs for the poor at every stage. As a side product, she provides information on environmental issues to areas where earlier there was hardly any interest in the topic and government programmes failed to reach the people. It might seem amazing that 98% of the inhabitants in 'her' neighbourhoods pay their waste disposal fees. The average payment rate usually achieved by the administration does not exceed 60%. This can probably be ascribed to the fact that the living standard of people goes up noticeably when the negative side effects of the refuse are reduced so dramatically. 'A pile of rubbish is a chance, not just a problem. Plastic, organic waste, cardboard – all that means money!' Albina said. She was beaming, and we were surprised that rubbish could excite so many positive emotions. However, Albina is not inspired by the refuse itself, but rather by the prospect of improving the quality of life of those for whom she developed the system. At this point, the system in Lima offers up to 50,000 jobs for the poorest of the poor and reaches three million people.

Clean cities all over the world

With the support of several foundations, Albina's concept has consequently been extended to several cities in South America and her consultation is being requested all over the world. This obviously means hard work. The drawn-out negotiations and discussions don't really suit Albina's temper: 'During difficult moments I take a deep breath and count from one to ten . . . or I get really angry and loud.'

In spite of that, Albina is content:

> The job is hard, but wonderful! Whenever a family gets money with the help of a junk-job and can buy fresh bread or send the kids to school, it is a wonderful feeling for me. Poor people are in need of my work, and I want to change the world for them. Some people don't have a bed and live on a pile of rubbish. Nevertheless, they get up and collect refuse, every day – their job is a lot harder than mine. My dream is to have clean cities all over the world. Maybe I won't be alive to see my dream come true, but I believe my children will. At this very moment, our model is being exported to Mexico and Uganda.

The light and the dark side of entrepreneurship

It is inevitable that we use the word 'radiant' in connection with Albina again and again; her whole nature seems to radiate and welcome the world as it comes. Her laughter lines make her look much younger than the age her daughter suggests. Despite her difficult path, Albina has probably always stayed the happy girl from the jungle inside. She has managed to balance a difficult job, not only with her family life, but also with her conviction that we have responsibility for others and are able to meet this responsibility in our everyday lives. However, the way has been long and trying: first Albina had to fight the prejudice against her job, then the corruption in the different administrative sections of the boroughs, while struggling repeatedly with problems of funding. Though the systems she developed do indeed operate cost-effectively, their development, documentation and expansion demand initial capital. The permanent search for money, the filing of applications, responding to requests and the tiring negotiations have left their mark in the last 15 years. Today, Albina is supported by several organisations for social entrepreneurship. In 2006, she was awarded the Skoll Award for Social Entrepreneurship and she will use the prize money she received – which amounts to US$500,000 – to export her system to 20 more cities.

With time, reputation settles in

This successful engineer of complex systems does not object to being called 'refuse queen'. After all, she creates hundreds of jobs, helps millions of people avoid sicknesses and horrendous health-care costs they can hardly afford, while beautifying their cities along the way. And even Albina's beloved jungle has shared in her commitment. In her home region she supports various projects, including, but not limited to, helping fund community buildings in which 3,000 women so far have found work in restaurants, craft shops, tourist shelters and other businesses. Hygienic waste disposal sites and schools for children are necessary there as well.

Today, when Albina gives reports about her experiences around the world or happens to be honoured by Robert Redford with a prize, it fits her life – just as much as leading her staff and coaching the technical development of her innovative systems do. As Albina told us, she would have never imagined all of this as a child, back in the jungle of Peru.

Information

- www.ciudadsaludable.org/en/index.html
- www.ashoka.org/node/3718
- www.schwabfound.org
- www.avina.net/eng

  Websites of organisations that have awarded and supported Albina for her social entrepreneurship.

- www.skollfoundation.org/entrepreneur/albina-ruiz

  The Skoll Foundation, initiated by eBay founder Jeff Skoll, has awarded Albina several years' worth of financial support in order to spread the model she developed internationally.

'Money itself has no value for me. I'm a successful business woman. But running my business only for the money would be awfully boring and, indeed, meaningless.'

Safia Minney
Media specialist, magazine
manager, fair-trade business
owner, fashion designer
Tokyo, Japan

Safia Minney – Fair trade – haute-couture: making beautiful clothes and making sense

Safia comes from the fast world of advertisement and glossy magazines. At the age of 17, the Londoner had no further interest in school and joined the investors' magazine of a traditional industry newspaper. After only six months she was bored, and the offer of an advertising agency came at just the right time. Even before she had properly started, she was called into the boss's office where she learned that for a long time the agency had been losing a lot of money on a wedding magazine.

Since Safia had worked at a magazine, albeit briefly, her employers wanted to give her the chance to make the wedding magazine profitable again. The ambitious young woman took on the challenge and, along with her team, actually managed to increase the print run of the magazine by seven times its original number within four years, consequently driving the publication far into the profit zone. During that time, she enjoyed the multicultural environment in the agency, gained more and more self-confidence and began going to school again.

Healed by a shock in far away land

Just as many other young people do, Safia also caught the desire to explore the world and travel for a longer period of time. Subsequently, she went to Bali and travelled from there by land to Myanmar (at that time called Burma). What she saw during her daily forays shocked her. In her high-gloss world, she had internalised common preconceptions about third-world countries. She had imagined those who lived there to be poor, pitiful slackers who spent their days sitting around waiting for charitable handouts. Instead, she found hard-working and talented people who manufactured excellent products with craft traditions that had been passed down over centuries. Of course, she also saw the miserable conditions under which many of them were forced to work. But above all, she realised that the customary cottage industries had neither the knowledge, nor the basic set-up, to sell their products internationally. In addition, the local demand was also quite low. Often, Safia was very upset when she heard the stories of people who, in spite of their very hard work, had no opportunity to gain a foothold in international competition. They had to struggle for the single dollar needed daily to be able to put a bowl of rice on the table for their families.

When dog food counts for more than people's lives

After almost a year of travel, Safia returned to London with a tremendous wealth of impressions. She could no longer understand why highly intelligent people spent their days thinking up the latest advertising tricks for things such as dog food and diets. She thought about the millions of dollars thrown away on these advertising battles, while images of people who had barely had enough to eat ran through her mind. For the first time, she asked herself seriously whether the skills of Londoners could be used in a more positive way.

Safia dived in head first and founded her own marketing consultancy. She specialised herself in consulting for charitable organisations, ethnic minorities and in building up and publicising her knowledge about topics that were important to her; such as foreign aid, feminism, ecology and human rights. For the first time, she was certain about why she got up every morning. However, when James, her boyfriend at the time and later her husband, received a very good job offer in Japan, they seized the opportunity and moved there. Safia, now 25, looked forward to the new cultural prospects and, in this way, Tokyo became Safia's new home.

Japan – a different world

And yet here a new slew of shocks were waiting for Safia – not only because of the new language and culture. She was very surprised when she discovered herself among Indian and Italian missionaries in her language school who wanted to care for the Japanese homeless in wealthy Japan. Tokyo, the proud high-tech metropolis, apparently did not concern itself with the not-so-successful members of society. Safia was even more astonished when she realised that she could find none of the information about organically grown food or fair-trade products that were common in Great Britain. Following her travel experiences, she had made it a habit in England to buy socially and ecologically conscious products. But in Japan, consuming in a socially and ecologically sustainable way seemed not to be an issue.

Foundation number 1 – Global Village

Safia's entrepreneurial spirit told her that she had to change something. So in 1989, she founded Global Village together with friends, a non-governmental organisation (NGO) which works for social and ecological justice. In the first years, Global Village concentrated itself on publicising information about socially and ecologically conscious shopping possibilities. Thanks to her husband, who earned a lot as a bank official, Safia had a much-too-large, mostly empty house at her disposal – ideal as a headquarters for Global Village. Filling the house with people who were working on something positive seemed to her to be the only way to not feel guilty about her prosperity. Often Safia had to chase her team members out of her daughter's bedroom late in the evenings because she wanted to put the child to bed at last. This set-up couldn't be permanent. So after ten years, the growing Global Village moved in 1999 to its own office.

Foundation number 2 – People Tree (formerly the Fair Trade Company)

Six years after the founding of Global Village more and more requests about recommended products were sent directly to Safia. For this reason she decided to found another business in Japan in 1995. Once again she put her creativity and communicative talent to excellent use and launched a new organisation, the Fair Trade Company which was subsequently renamed People Tree. Since then, she has shown with People Tree that fair-trade consumer articles are on par with other products in terms of quality and design. Thanks to a continually rising demand for People Tree's products, over the last ten years she has been successful in building up a team of almost 60 partners who make sales of more than US$8 million per year in Japan, England, Switzerland, the USA and Italy. Aside from the conventional commerce in fair-trade products, which still make up the majority of its sales revenue, Safia has expanded the range of goods that the company creates by specialising herself more and more in the ecologically and socially conscious production of couture.

People Tree and its demands

In the latter half of 2005, we met Safia in her office in a suburb of Tokyo. Outside the language which she spoke almost perfectly after having lived there for the last 15 years, there is not much about her that is typically Japanese. She grew up in London as the daughter of an Indian-Mauritanian father and a Swiss mother. Safia is a petite woman who is full of energy; when we met, her black curls framed her often smiling face, and she was noticeably well-dressed. Simple, elegant and somewhat youthful – all fair trade, she clarified.

Under the People Tree label, Safia coordinates 70 groups of producers in 20 countries. Her teams in both the London-based design centre and in Japan develop international, high-fashion articles of clothing which are then manufactured by these relatively small groups all around the world. This way it becomes possible for tailors in remote Laos or the South American jungle to sell products on the world market. Quality is the highest imperative: all of the goods have to hold their own in the market against conventionally manufactured articles, whose manufacture is often also bad for the environment. Japan still does not offer the luxury of fair trade to enlightened customers. Safia has built up suitable local producers primarily in the developing world. She has made additional education possible for many of them and shown them how fashions are worn in Japan and in the world. In conversation Safia explained,

> Many of our Peruvian workers wake up at four in the morning in order to manufacture a piece for our collection before they have to care for their children. It's not always easy to make clear to them why one centimetre more or less can be extremely decisive for People Tree's customers. Or to explain to them why the colours of each piece must look exactly the same. For all that, I am grateful to know that a woman like that can nourish her family and send her children to school. For that reason I'm happy to work a little bit more.

Free market?

Of course People Tree takes care of marketing for the products that are produced abroad. Safia knows all too well that it is impossible for small manufacturers to make their way in today's free market. As she said,

> A free market is among other things a market with perfect information. When I think about how bad the information about the ecological and social consequences of the manufacture of many products still is, I don't think we can speak about free markets with regard to this.

Even high-ranking decision-makers in politics and industry don't know with certainty about the consequences they are responsible for. She realised this with horror when she attended the World Economic Forum in Davos. As she sees it, the leaders of today lack access to some very critical information. Safia was convinced that, 'even consumers are being manipulated very cleverly by well-paid public relations (PR) and marketing professionals. They're pulling the wool over people's eyes.' People Tree in contrast, wants to enlighten and enable consumers to make conscious purchasing decisions.

Challenge for the manufacturers

As long as the social and ecological costs of manufacturing goods are not included in their prices, what goes on internationally cannot be considered to be free competition in free markets. Ecological and social requirements would have to be anchored in the legal framework of production much more than it currently is. As an example, Safia cites cotton production. Cotton is traditionally grown with intensive use of water and pesticides. In many regions water is very scarce and the cotton plantations see to it that the reserves are used up even more quickly. More than 20,000 fieldworkers in cotton production die annually due to exposure to poisonous pesticides, leaving their families behind without income. People Tree works only with organically produced cotton, but they must still, however, count on a higher price. As Safia told us:

> Just the fact that this cotton must be ordered and paid for eight to 16 months before its use makes it impossible for many of our workers to access raw materials for their production without the support of People Tree.

Her desire to help people overcome this and other problems that are a consequence today's economic system drives Safia to succeed.

Fair trade has to be sexy

She wants to help fair trade gain a modern image. 'Fair-trade couture was ugly and old-fashioned ten years ago. Today we have the ability to create very attractive fashions,' she insisted, and showed us a few garments from the next collection. They were being developed in the next room by top designers that she won over for People Tree. Safia and her team are convinced that high quality, fair-trade fashions can be brought to stores at reasonable prices.

> There are excellent fair-trade fabrics. Why shouldn't we be able to make sexy clothes out of them? Of course we need professionals for that. We get them, too. Our design centre in London is practically under siege by successful designers who are looking to make their work meaningful.

Money itself has no meaning

Safia enthused:

> The longer I work in fair trade and the deeper my insight into global relationships gets, the more convinced I am about our work at People Tree. Just the positive effects for the people in our partner projects show me that the hard work of the past years has been worthwhile. I can't even describe the joy and inner satisfaction that you feel when you meet these people.

Safia could earn much more than she does at big fashion labels or well-known magazines, but that doesn't interest her. 'I wouldn't be any happier if I were richer. In my life it's always been about principles and values,' she told us. Trade – and its accompanying information – is a powerful tool for Safia in making people socially and politically mature, and giving them a voice. However in most large businesses, social responsibility and ecological stewardship are only at home in the PR department. 'It's going to take many years before these subjects are anchored in core industry,' Safia feared. She sees one of her tasks as speeding up this process through the example of her own success.

Information

- www.peopletree.co.uk
  People Tree's website.

- www.globalvillage.or.jp
  Japanese NGO Global Village, which engages itself for ecological and social justice and was founded by Safia Minney.

- www.helvetas.ch
  Founded in 1955 as the first private development organisation in Switzerland, Helvetas is known for strong engagement in the area of organic cotton.

- www.gepa.de
  GEPA is the largest fair-trade organisation in Europe.

- www.fairtrade-deuschland.de
  Information portal on fair trade run by Transfair, which was founded in 1992 with the mission of supporting disadvantaged manufacturing families in Africa, Asia and Latin America through fair trade.

- www.maxhavelaar.org
  The Max Havelaar Foundation supports fair relationships worldwide.

'What's important is what you're going to look back on when you're on your deathbed. Can you imagine thinking to yourself then: "Oh, if only I had spent more time in the office!"?'

Chris Eyre
Finance specialist, basketball team manager, philanthropy consultant, family man
Palo Alto, California, USA

Chris Eyre – A very different kind of venture capital

For many people, the pursuit of a successful career in high finance and the improvement of our world seem to be mutually exclusive. Either you can use your abilities for earning a lot of money, or you can use them for making positive change. Both of these together just don't seem possible.

The Harvard priorities

Chris Eyre once surely belonged to those who are convinced of this assumption, or who never even asked themselves the question of whether compatibility was possible. Growing up in the American state of Utah, family and religion had been very important to Chris throughout his life. However, these values waned for some time after he graduated from Harvard. Studying business at an elite American university is like having a one-way ticket to big money. Starting with his first job, Chris landed a bull's eye: he had the chance to work with colleagues to develop the venture capital branch of Bank of America, one of the USA's biggest banks.

Venture capital and phenomenal profits

At that time, venture capital was a relatively unknown type of asset: banks invest in the early stages of risky ventures with their own capital. If the investor selects the right businesses, the invested capital could increase multiple times within only a few years, allowing the investment to be sold at a very high price. Even if some of the start-up businesses never manage to make it to breakthrough, the profit of the successful ones more than make up for the possible losses.

At the beginning of the 1970s, Chris founded one of the first independent venture-capital firms in the renowned Silicon Valley along with three partners: Merill, Pickar, Anderson & Eyre. The partners collected money for a fund which they used to invest in early technology start-ups. Since they did this at exactly the right time and at the beginning of the coming boom in the field, they were soon able to report fantastic profits. The success had, however, its dark side: the work days were long, and it was not uncommon that Chris himself went to a meeting after 13 intensive work hours in order to hear how yet another team of enthusiastic entrepreneurs thought they would develop the next multimillion-dollar venture.

But what about the rest?

Even though Chris enjoyed his work a lot, he noticed how his life became more and more one-sided. Above all, his family suffered under the permanent shortage of time. During our conversation he pensively recalled one decisive moment, shortly before his 40th birthday. He was sitting late in the evening with a team that wanted to bring the next electronic super-toy out onto the market. As his thoughts rambled wearily, he realised that he had – as had often happened in the last few years – once again missed one of his son's basketball games.

This was the deciding moment in which Chris resolved to change something in his life. The idea that he might one day lie on his deathbed without having had time for his family and the truly important things in life had become unbearable. Ultimately, it was because of these thoughts that he developed the sense that he wanted to do something meaningful for other people. 'What's important is what you're going to look back on when you're on your deathbed. Can you imagine thinking to yourself then: "Oh, if only I had spent more time in the office!"?'

At that point, Chris could not count on the understanding of his colleagues. They called him crazy and shook their heads. Yet, his decision to get out persisted. Even the thought of missing out on the million-dollar profits (which the boom in the field made very likely) did not deter him from his course.

Time for family and more

The transition to a new life phase was difficult for Chris. His job had put him in contact with many interesting entrepreneurs and their innovative business models. His work had also been connected with respect, renown and a copious salary. Since Chris voluntarily no longer worked in a paid job, he had to dispense with many of these advantages. In spite of this, his new life felt good. Not only did he have time for his son's basketball games, he could even manage the team. Beyond this, Chris became intensely engaged in his church community and enjoyed the time that he suddenly had free for his family and other interests. Finally he was no longer driven by the next appointment, but could instead do exactly what he wanted to do. It was of no concern that he had to live on savings; enough money had accrued over the years.

It didn't take long however, until Chris was nagged by the question of whether he was using his skills optimally in his current commitments. He frequently asked himself, 'Am I really realising my maximum positive contribution to the world with what I'm doing?' Although he was sometimes very satisfied, he sometimes had the feeling that he could undertake something more with all of his contacts and knowledge. Chris's children were getting older, so when one of his former business partners underwent a similar change in sentiments and offered Chris a new idea, it came exactly at the right time.

The perfect offer

The new idea was about creating an intelligent connection between the world of earning money and the world of global improvement. Chris could not resist. The idea foresaw using both of their relationships, built up over the years, for the best venture-capital companies in the USA to give affluent people the chance to do well – and in a very professional way. With this goal, Legacy Venture was founded in 1999.

Wealthy people invested money into the legacy funds. Chris and his partner placed this money in the best venture-capital funds. These are normally so successful and in such demand that new investors can hardly gain access to them. The venture-capital funds used the money they amassed to buy shares in promising, early-stage business ventures in medical and technology fields. After a few years these shares were sold for a multiple of what they were originally worth, generating very high yields. These yields flowed back to Legacy Venture and the affluent investors. The decisive point was, however, that the investors pledged beforehand to devote these profits to initiatives which make the world better and create solutions for serious social and ecological problems. Chris helps his investors select projects, which he evaluates with a rigour and professionalism that is comparable to his earlier work in investment. The difference today, however, is that he tries to maximise social and ecological profits, not the financial ones.

The profits are donated and the investors can claim tax deductions on these donations in accordance with American tax law. Thus, Legacy Venture creates a unique system that provides great benefits – above all for the socially-conscious organisations it supports. They profit from large donations and also from the invaluable business experience and relationships which are also brought into the cooperation.

The privilege of networking

After a having spent a few years at Legacy, Chris remarked to us at the interview:

> I have the rare privilege of working with the most incredible entrepreneurs in the non-profit sector. They are the true business people of our world – 'social entrepreneurs', who use their passion and their confidence to make the world a better place. When I can

put them in contact with generous, talented philanthropists, this combination creates amazingly positive energy.

Chris is also happy that he has been able to make the change in accordance with his lifestyle:

> Before you do something really meaningful, you've got to be both healthy and happy with yourself. My personal philosophy is: make sure you're ok first. Second priority has to be your family. The third priority – independent of religious belief – is our fellow human beings, which in my opinion simply is a broader definition of family.

A clever combination with profits for all

Through deft bridge-building between the non-profit and for-profit world, Chris is creating a so-called 'quadruple profit situation'. First, of course, the Legacy Venture model benefits charitable organisations and the people they serve. Second, the charitable donations of the Legacy Venture investors receive a significant boost through the Legacy Venture model, and the effect of the positive contribution is greatly increased. Third, even if it seems less obvious, the managers of the venture-capital funds are happy because a portion of their work is dedicated with certainty to a good cause. And not least, Chris enjoys his work, which he can connect to many of his skills and ideals. Today, he is very happy that he had the courage to resist the temptations of the typical career path.

The 'who's who' of Silicon Valley

Chris very much enjoys working with the 'who's who' of the most successful business people in Silicon Valley. These are not just the innovative movers behind companies such as Cisco, Yahoo and Google. More than that, many of them are also very passionate philanthropists, who are not merely concerned with filling out the next cheque and using it to buy peace of mind. Actively assisting the projects they support financially is an important concern for them. They want to help these beneficial organisations successfully grow – and in the most efficient and effective way possible. Chris considers it an honour to work with and for these people, and he always enjoys seeing the passion in their eyes when they are able to engage themselves in a positive cause.

At the conclusion of our conversation, Chris explained: 'I have a lot of trust in the capitalist system. I still believe that it does more good than bad. Legacy

Venture uses the purest parts of this system – entrepreneurs and venture capital – to do good.'

Information

- www.legacyventure.com
  Legacy Venture's website.

- www.evpa.eu.com
  European Venture Philanthropy Association: A federation of European organisations engaged in the field of venture philanthropy or social-venture capital.

- www.bonventure.de/en/home.html

'Every business decision
also has social and
ecological consequences.
Business doesn't operate
in a vacuum.'

Maria Emilia Correa
Sociologist, nature lover,
environmental activist,
business executive
Santiago de Chile, Chile

Maria Emilia Correa – From critiquing business to taking responsibility

On our trip around five continents, we spoke with many business managers who were leading the world in ecological and social areas. For example, Toyota impressed us not only with the socially responsible and ecologically forward-looking management of its production sites, but also with its now well-known hybrid vehicles. We talked with managers at Xerox about, among other things, a recycling concept developed and implemented for the Asian and Australian region. Today the business can dismantle and re-use 99.1% of all printer parts in its own factories. This process saves material and energy, creates jobs and is now also not to be overlooked as a source of income. Interestingly, thoughts about this cycle have also led to important impulses for development and innovation, leading to better quality and interesting customer contacts.

Even the electronics concern, Philips, satisfied us with its new strategy, a completely new series of products called 'Eco-Heroes', to be developed and produced in compliance with the highest possible ecological standards. We knew already that Japan, which for years has focused on high-end technology, is also a leader in the area of ecological innovation. It was even more exciting to find an example of such innovation in South America, particularly because Grupo Nueva, which we visited, is, among other things, involved in the lumber industry, a business branch which is best known in the region for deforestation of rain forests and inhumane work conditions.

A typical business?

In the beautiful wood-built headquarters of Grupo Nueva in Santiago de Chile, we were received by Maria Emilia Correa in early 2006. A woman in her late 40s who has, since the year 2000, been in charge of social and ecological responsibility as a vice president of the company. Her office was modern and flooded with natural light. On a bow-shaped desk stood a neat row of all of today's necessary work tools: a laptop with a wireless keyboard, a telephone and an electronic day calendar. A modern art piece in red decorated the wall.

Grupo Nueva is a holding group for businesses operating in Latin America; for example, one member firm deals in water treatment systems, another is a construction material enterprise and Masisa is a concern in the area of lumber production and processing. The group was founded by Stephan Schmidheiny, a Swiss entrepreneur who has been engaged for years in sustainable economic development in Latin America. This man is the one who convinced Maria Emilia, through many conversations and provocative questions, that big business is the right place to work for improving the world. Schmidheiny is at least a decade ahead of the rest of the world with his concept of sustainability, not only in his publications, but also in his business practices. His holding group clearly shows how to achieve business management practically in terms of a triple profit: that means financial, social and ecological success. It was on this basis, Maria Emilia told us, that her position, among others, was created in the year 2000. Since then, she and the team of Grupo Nueva have implemented as many changes as possible which she had earlier in life demanded from businesses as a nature conservationist in her home country of Columbia.

Sociology and activism

Maria Emilia completed a legal degree at the end of the 1970s at the University of Bogotá. Even then she was very interested in the social aspects of human coexistence. She would have liked to have studied sociology, but in Columbia this subject had fallen into disrepute due to its revolutionary gloss. So instead she focused on social considerations in the study of law and later decided to add on another master's degree in sociology and social history from the New School for Social Research in New York. After she returned home in 1984, she was unexpectedly offered a job in environmental protection. The young woman took the job primarily because of her personal love of nature. She became involved with questions of the protection of natural resources and biodiversity for organisations such as The Nature Conservancy and Fundación Natura, among others.

Business power can work for good

Directly following the world summit in Rio de Janeiro in 1992, Maria Emilia was asked by the World Business Council for Sustainable Development (WBCSD) whether she was interested in writing a book and developing and implementing a seminar series with the theme 'Sustainability and Business in Latin America'. Pleased at the honour of being able to support Latin America on its path towards a sustainable economy and society, Maria Emilia crisscrossed the continent as a consultant over the next few years.

It was during this work that she met Stephan Schmidheiny, who had started the World Business Council for the world summit in Rio and edited some important publications. Maria Emilia recalled:

> As I read the book *Changing Course* by Stephan Schmidheiny in 1992, his idea that business could be the driving power for positive change was completely new for me. This thought was completely contrary to the mindset of the conservationists, who saw

'businesses' as the enemy. Today I see it like this: the role of the civil society, activists and conservationists is still to put critical topics onto the agendas of politicians and businesses. However, in this role one can change only very little. In contrast, inside business, you're in the right position to implement positive development – even when it's sometimes difficult.

Thus Maria Emilia, inspired by Schmidheiny's book, endeavoured to make clear to businesses the power and responsibilities they have in society. This responsibility was not limited to generating higher profits, but extended to generating and utilising profits in a way which promotes people's quality of living and which, at the least, does not worsen the environmental situation.

Maria Emilia as a business critic

Maria Emilia's consulting work culminated directly in a five-year stint as the leader of the WBCSD in Columbia. In this function she was able to oppose various developments made by individual businesses directly and critically. Together with international partners of the WBCSD, she developed new concepts and ideas and attempted to implement them in member businesses. In this way she assisted, for example, in bringing topics such as corporate social responsibility (CSR), and resource efficiency onto the agenda for international business:

> If you want to speak to a business as an environmental conservationist, you start down a path on which you must learn two languages. This path also requires a strong component of trust and respect. And then things run as they do in any other negotiation situation that strives for a profit for both sides: you take a little and you give a little.

Apparently, Maria Emilia understood how to manage the different languages and ways of thinking so well that the chief executive officer (CEO) of Grupo Nueva, Julio Moura, approached her in 2000 and offered her the newly created position of vice president for environmental and social affairs.

Maria Emilia as a business woman

Maria Emilia said to us,

> In the years before 2000, I criticised businesses from outside and tried to show them what they could change. And now, suddenly, I sat on the important decision-making body of a corporate group with 11,000 workers and realised how difficult it was to implement

many of the best concepts in reality. When I started at Grupo Nueva,[11] I had no clue about business management; I didn't know the rules and understood little of the challenges. Today I understand them and I also know the potential at the disposal of businesses is to achieve change.

Maria Emilia gratefully remembers the support of Julio Moura, who inducted her into the foundations – and later into the subtler rules – of the game of business management. Thanks to this introduction she was more frequently able to make her ideas a reality. In particular, she managed to initiate a cultural transformation over the years. This succeeded through ongoing clarification and communication, but above all, through the fact that she made social and ecological criteria firm components of all investment decisions. These criteria were also consistently modelled in the strategic decisions of the business management – only this way the efforts were credible. In conversation she explained:

> Every business decision also has a social and ecological dimension. Business doesn't operate in a vacuum. Managers are trained to think about financial ratios for hours at a time, illuminate them, optimise them, consider the smallest variables involved. At the same time they are making decisions about the living situation of hundreds of families in five seconds, or they don't question the water, air and soil pollution caused by their choices. With us that's radically changing. Today no business decision can be made without considering the ecological and social consequences.

Voluntary observance of standards

We wanted to know what concrete measures Grupo Nueva has taken because of her work, she told us:

> For example, we hold ourselves voluntarily to the highest European standards in the formaldehyde content of our lumber panels. This standard, which is not required by our markets, costs us $6 million each year, which we have to save somewhere else. Despite this, we are convinced that this is the best decision for our customers and workers. In order to make it good for business too, we try to use such measures for marketing purposes.

These and similar sensible restrictions which the business has placed on itself are, based on Maria Emilia's experience, a source of innovation that should

---

11 The Grupo Nueva aimed to increase its sales volume from US$674 million to US$1,700 million and its earnings before interest, taxes, depreciation and amortisation from US$62 million to US$260 million between 2001 and 2006.

not be underestimated. Ever more often, it's possible to earn back the costs through better solutions in other areas of the business.

A special legal structure for maintaining values

It is interesting that Grupo Nueva carries out its environmental and social measures not just as a special programme on the margin of the core business, but instead tries to integrate these principles everywhere. In order to promote this, Stephan Schmidheiny developed a special legal structure. The main stockholder of Grupo Nueva is the VIVA Trust, a trust company that is meant to guarantee that all of the group's business is carried out in a socially and ecologically responsible way. Portions of the profits are used to finance Avina, a network for Latin American social entrepreneurs. The VIVA Trust sees to it that the vision and the values of the founders are lived out by all of its organisations.

Integration into the core business

We wondered how such thoughts were manifested through the core business. Maria Emilia names as an example a strategic standard that she enacted together with the chief executive: at least 10% of all the sales of Grupo Nueva must be generated by projects which improve the quality of life of their most financially disadvantaged customers in a targeted and active way. In order to promote the creativity of the employees, these projects must also generate the usual profit yield. This standard, according to Maria Emilia, has allowed the creation of many new approaches in the last few years. Since the solutions must have a broad range of application, some ideas have to be eliminated, but others have been implemented very successfully in recent years. For example, the irrigation machine division developed a drip-irrigation system for small farmers in Guatemala. This system was tailored to the local average size of cultivation areas and is therefore only half as expensive as conventional systems. Because Grupo Nueva also allows farmers with access to credit, this innovative irrigation system could be sold in high numbers. On the one hand, this is good for Grupo Nueva's stockholders, while on the other, water use in Guatemala was sharply reduced and the crop yield of small farmers increased.

Good profit for a good cause

Maria Emilia was visibly happy as she recalled this work:

> Creating such positive changes for all stakeholders allows me to wake up happy every day. Profit is a good thing, if you can initiate good projects with it. As a business, we of course have a final responsibility towards our stockholders. It's not our money; we can't simply give it away. Our investments in environmental improvement and social responsibility are, on the one hand, risk management for our business. On the other hand, they are a bet placed on the markets and customer demands developing in this direction. We are completely convinced that customers will reward ecologically and socially sensitive business practices with their purchase decisions, and so we would like, of course, to create win-win situations ahead of our competition.

Maria Emilia explained this to us with the quick-wittedness of a woman who has learned to understand the needs of different people and stakeholders, and to use the right language with each.

People are worth more than machines

The stress of the life of a top manager is enormous. Yet the positive results that can be achieved in such a position make up for a lot, she believes. It becomes ever more apparent that the employees of Grupo Nueva are proud of their employer. Outstanding, skilled workers purposefully apply themselves to the company because it is known for the values it practices. Maria Emilia is very happy that the employees of Grupo Nueva don't have to check their consciences at the door.

Yet there are also other experiences that give her work routine meaning:

> For example when I began working with Amanco, our company that produces water systems, on their accident rate in production, they were considerably over the branch average. After we had implemented all of our programmes, we had significantly reduced the number of accidents and had brought them considerably under the branch average. Those are the numbers. Behind the numbers there are people who have been kept healthy. I found myself again at a point where I knew exactly what I got up for every morning when an employee came to me and, after announcing these numbers, said with bright eyes: 'For the first time, I feel like I'm worth more than our machines.

According to Maria Emilia, her basic motivation has not changed significantly in the last decades:

My inspiration comes from two things: first and foremost is my basic love of nature. I simply love enjoying the mountains, woods, lakes and the plant and animal world. Then there is also the social construct, the fact that the environment is the foundation of all human life and, on top of that, an arena for many social interactions.

Bracing for the future

How can the past year's paradigm shift, which Maria Emilia and the executive team of Grupo Nueva successfully introduced, be anchored so that it can endure in the future? How can values be institutionalised so that they will live on, even when the people who once propagated them are no longer there? Maria Emilia asks herself often how much of her hard work would endure if the pressure from executives and her were to let up. She cannot yet answer these questions satisfactorily. She summed up her current attitude once more:

> Businesses form society and businesses are a social act. Each decision made by a manager has an effect, most often a negative one. I'm not saying that we shouldn't make any decisions. We should give ourselves a few minutes of time to consider their consequences and to find ways we can have less negative or even positive effects.

Since Maria Emilia has striven over decades in different positions to order her life and work so that it does not violate her own basic principles, she was, however, quite sure:

> We won't be in a position to solve today's problems with the same mode of thinking which created those problems. That's the reason why it is so important to work with young people and expand their horizons. To show them that all of their activities in business have ecological and social repercussions and that this represents not only a great risk, but also a great opportunity.

Information

- www.vivatrust.com/home/?lid=2

  Website of Grupo Nueva.

- www.vivatrust.com

  The VIVA Trust finances the activities of the Avina Foundation and other philanthropic initiatives which strive for the sustainable development of society with a portion of the dividends generated by Grupo Nueva.

- www.wbcsd.org

  An association of businesses devoted to sustainable development founded by Stephan Schmidheiny in 1992.

- www.avina.net/eng

  South American network of social entrepreneurs.

- www.stephanschmidheiny.net

CONCLUSION

The following represent what we consider to be five of the most important insights and experiences from Chapter 1:

1. You can use almost every professional background to make the world more beautiful, more liveable and more sustainable

2. Many seemingly too specific skills turn out to be highly valuable in the field of social innovation and lead to creative and unique solutions

3. An increasing amount of social innovation work is done across sectors, industries and functions – experience from multiple perspectives is highly valuable, while the ability to cooperate is absolutely key

4. You can fill the gaps in technical knowledge in smart and efficient ways. Continuous education, reading and through exchange, help to expand competences and abilities

5. Personal balance and well-being – often attained through experience in other fields – is the prerequisite for the ability to initiate positive change for others

2

'I'm too young or too old'

'I am far too young for that. Although, I would like to face this challenge, I am lacking the experience.' Does such a statement sound familiar to you? There are many obstacles that seem to stand in the way when realising professional ideals or dreams when you are young. First your vocational training or studies call for graduation and, in order to secure your material needs, it is necessary to earn enough money. In the further process of building a career there are decisive steps that need to be given consideration and the standard of life that one achieves should be maintained.

The spiral keeps turning and, in spite of covert dissatisfaction, there is a strong temptation never to leave the path you set on – for reasons of comfort, out of fear of the unknown or because there are financial obligations to be met. As a consequence, the realisation of your real longing and visions are delayed again and again, until you feel too old for the adventure of making a new start.

The stories presented in Chapter 2 show that it is possible to reset or transform the tracks at every stage in life. These accounts want to encourage and clarify: our age does not define when in life what we can do. It lies in our own hands – to a substantial degree – how we shape our lives, no matter if you are 20 or 60 years old.

An example is Mia Hanak, who – at a very young age – founded the Natural World Museum shortly after her graduation. Or a man like Dr V who was 80 when he still performed eye surgery on the poorest of the poor in India. 'You don't retire as long as people are suffering. What does retirement even mean?' he liked to say.

'I had the chance to help, so I did. You don't retire as long as people are suffering. What does retirement even mean?'

Dr V†
Ophthalmologist, retirement-refusenik, family head, visionary
Madurai, India

Dr V – The McDonaldisation of eye surgery

Discussion of retirement in the western industry seems absurd when looking at Dr Gonvindappa Venkataswamy's (or simply Dr V's) lifework. As we met the 88 year old in his ophthalmology clinic at Aravind Eye Care headquarters in southern Madurai towards the middle of 2005, he recounted in a calm and serene manner, 'I had the chance to help, so I did. You don't retire when there are people suffering. What does retirement even mean?' Until he died in the autumn of 2006, Dr V arrived at his ophthalmology clinic every morning at 7 am to further his vision of obliterating unnecessary blindness in the world. So, it is not surprising that he was admired, not only by his family and the millions of poor people whom he had helped, but also by eye specialists from around the world.

Why did everything begin at the age of 58?

It was a valid question to ask why Dr V, who was born in 1918 in a poor village in southern India, started to build up Aravind at the seemingly late age of 58 and not earlier. Dr V lost his father at 16 and, as the eldest son, was forced to take responsibility for his family. He became a medic in the Indian military after receiving medical training from Stanley Medical College in 1944. Unfortunately, he had to interrupt his career after four years because he suffered from chronic rheumatoid arthritis. This illness permanently crippled his fingers. Dr V told us, 'It always had been my dream to help the village people – people who had, for one reason or another, lost their eyesight, and had no opportunity to regain it, because the hospitals do not even have enough beds'.

Dr V's fighting nature

Dr V did not let his unfavourable life circumstances stand in the way that easily. Despite his debilitating disability, he enrolled as a medical student again and completed his training as a medical specialist in ophthalmology. Practice using the surgical instruments cost him many hours because his crippled fingers forced him to hold the instruments at a special angle. He nevertheless perfected the technique in the course of his life, consequently liberating 100,000 people from cataracts. First, however, Dr V became the director of ophthalmology at the medical college in Madurai and he soon became known for finding innovative ways to combat blindness.

Do 50 million people have to be blind?

Blindness is a disease which even today destroys the lives of almost 50 million people worldwide. In India alone, blindness makes a dignified life almost impossible for 12 million people. In a country very rich and utterly poor at the same time, and filled with challenges, many people must make ends meet with less than US$1 a day. In such cases, as an Indian saying goes, a blind person is indeed a mouth without hands. Once blind, it is practically impossible to continue working in one's trade. A blind person further encumbers the already strongly burdened family. Research has indeed shown that people who lose their eyesight in developing nations rarely live for more than two to three years. Despite this, 80% of all eye diseases that lead to blindness in India are curable. However, Dr V was very aware from his own experience that the transportation costs alone to the nearest hospital are simply unaffordable for many people in rural India, not to mention the costs of hospital care or surgery. Health insurance is only available to the very rich through private means. For this reason, Dr V had already initiated aid programmes during his time at the college. Under his supervision, eye doctors drove into rural areas to help people locally. He trained ordinary people as ophthalmology assistants, who could at least conduct preliminary examinations in remote villages. Especially close to his heart was saving children from becoming blind due to malnutrition.

Retirement as the beginning of a new life

Once they reach the age of retirement, many make it their goal to bridge the time until they die with going on holiday, golfing, watching television and other pastimes. But, for Dr V, the beginning of retirement brought the opportunity to fulfil his dream. First of all, he wanted to perfect the surgical removal of cataracts, which are by far the leading cause of unnecessary blindness, so that the operation would be as safe, simple and affordable as a burger at McDonald's. Or, as Dr V expressed it, 'We are interested in selling the product of "good sight" to those people for whom sight is essential to survival. We can organise the cataract operation in developing nations in a way that makes it affordable for anyone.'

Dr V involved the majority of his own family as he began to build the first Aravind-Hospital for ophthalmology in 1976. He had, after all, also cared for his relatives, supporting them throughout their education, which many of them providentially completed in the field of ophthalmology.

> In 1977 I did not have the money to build hospitals; the banks said my credit was not good enough. For that reason, I took out a mortgage on my home. In the beginning, my brother had to sell a piece of jewellery here and there so that we would have enough to eat.

But then we succeeded in making a profit on the first floor of the
clinic and we were able to finish building the rest of it.

What began in 1976 with 11 beds and a great vision has now become the
world's biggest and most productive business of mass operations for cataract
patients. In more than 1,500 screening outposts in rural regions of India, 2.5
million people are checked every year for vision problems. Most of them can
be helped locally with used glasses and small operations. In Mandurai, about
200,000 patients with cataracts are operated on every year.

All of this only became financially feasible through optimisation of all the
processes involved. Today the sections support each other perfectly. Finally,
Aravind took the production of lenses into their own hands. Lenses that once
cost €150 per lens can be produced today with the help of an American company for only €3.50. In the meantime, Aravind exports these high-quality
lenses to 80 countries. The Aravind Clinic also streamlined the process of the
cataract operation. The operating ophthalmologist concentrates solely on
the operation; everything else is taken care of by numerous, well-educated
assistants.

With these specially developed techniques, the doctors are able to con-
duct up to 100 operations a day. This quality and efficiency is unparalleled
worldwide. Aravind is running five hospitals and, in addition, has established
'Vision Centres' and 'Community Centres' in some regions of India. In addition, it has a training centre that is accredited worldwide and exports its
model to the world by cooperating with 150 training hospitals.

Turning a profit when two-thirds of patients are treated for free

Every day, 600–1,000 people in Madurai undergo cataract surgery. It is spectacular that Dr V designed his system from the beginning so that two-thirds
of all patients can receive free treatment, while the clinic still earns enough
profit to expand. The operations at Aravind are free – and so are the vision
screenings in the villages, transportation to and from the village and the stay
and care in the hospital. The decision whether to pay or not is left to each
individual patient and there has never been envy or disputes as a result.
Every patient knows that everyone receives the same quality of treatment.
Those patients who pay do have better accommodation, however, Dr V said,
'One does not have to qualify for the free treatment. In the first place, I am not
operating a business here, but giving people back their vision and, with that,
I also give them back their lives'.

The joy of creating something wonderful

During our meeting, Dr V told us:

> My personal motivation and satisfaction stems from the circumstance of being able to help many people regain their vision. This is why it is so important to me that we share all of our knowledge with those who want it.

As we saw the line of people who were queuing in the hospital and subsequently the many patients taking the buses homeward who were full of joy over their recovered vision, we began to understand what Dr V meant.

As we sat across from him in his modest office, we hoped that in the future there would be many people – especially older people – who would feel inspired by his example:

> Intelligence and skill are not enough for this work. They have to be paired with the joy of accomplishing something wonderful. Helping humanity means more than using the most elaborate, best technology to truly serve the means to feel generosity and sympathy for every patient.

After these words, Dr V took us to visit his sister, Dr Nachiar, and his nephew, Dr Aravind, who came back to Madurai in order to continue his uncle's legacy after earning his MBA at Stanford.

The next generation

After that inspiring conversation, we also wanted to know what the next generation thought about this project. We already knew that his 30-year-old nephew had done more than use his skills as an eye surgeon for years in Madurai. He had also completed postgraduate studies in economics at one of the best American universities. What motivated this young person, who had the whole world at his feet, to return to Madurai? In answer to that question he told us,

> To take just any job only to earn lots of money was never really an option for me. I wanted to come back because my experiences in the USA made it even clearer to me what a great difference I can make for many people. Moreover, I have the unique opportunity here as a hospital manager to implement my entrepreneurial capabilities and simultaneously work as an eye surgeon. I love both of these professions.

Dr Aravind did not hesitate as we again asked where he saw the greatest differences between Dr V's approach and the business approach at Stanford:

> At Stanford I learned a lot about competitiveness, about how one creates a win-lose situation and goes on to win. Dr V gets people to think about life in a different manner. He crafts a vision together with them – a dream – and creates situations in which everyone wins.

He can identify much better with this attitude. This culture in their enterprise has made it possible for three generations with very different personalities to work together.

Everyone agrees about what Aravind's goal is. The next step is the expansion of activities so that a million operations a year are possible. The self-run hospitals – as well as cooperation with other hospitals – will make this possible. Above all, it is critical to maintain the values and quality that are the foundation of the company. But, with regard to this point, the whole Aravind family is very optimistic.

We are confident after these conversations that Dr V's legacy is in good hands. Step by step, his vision of eliminating unnecessary blindness from the world is now being implemented, even though he is not able to experience this after having built up Aravind for 30 years.

Information

- www.aravind.org
- www.aravindeyefoundation.org

  The Aravind Eye Foundation, formerly the Friends of Aravind, supports Aravind by networking, building partnerships with academic institutions and sharing best practices with other eye care facilities. The website also includes case studies on Aravind.

'It's the same everywhere in the world: a good quality of education is the foundation on which society is built. What really brings me peace though, is knowing that I have the opportunity to better the school system. I have the chance to improve the education children receive in many communities.'

Vicky Colbert de Arboleda
Sociologist, deputy of education, UNICEF-director, foundation founder
Bogotá, Colombia

Vicky Colbert de Arboleda – Education not drugs

For many Europeans, Colombia is still the land of the drug lords, the epitome of instability, violence and danger. In the early part of 2006, we landed at the airport in Bogotá with these same assumptions in mind, but were pleasantly surprised during the drive to our hotel. Outside of the car window, we saw numerous bike riders in noticeably clean bicycle lanes. The lanes set aside for bike riders are even wider than those reserved for cars, which upset our taxi driver. What upset him even more though, was that every Monday he had to let the bikers take over the entire narrow inner city roads. We did not expect to see so much nature and so many smiling families taking bicycle trips in this Latin American metropolis. Later, we learned that these developments are the results of the tenure of a former mayor, a visionary named Enrique Peñalosa.[12]

In the following days, we familiarised ourselves with Bogotá's new buildings and stores, which are part of the modern district's housing for some of the city's eight million people. In the city's quiet corners it is possible to sip a perfectly prepared espresso, visit the Gold Museum, or enjoy fresh sushi in one of the city's many sushi restaurants. However, what impressed us most were the friendly, optimistic and energetic people. Vicky Colbert de Arboleda is one of these people, always seen with an infectious smile on her face. She calmly explained to us the discrepancy between the reputation and reality of Colombia: 'There is a lot of entrepreneurship in Colombia – sometimes it takes a negative direction, but more often than not a positive one.' Vicky was also the one who reminded us of the low living standards in the poor districts, especially the disastrous quality of education – with education being the foundation for and a prerequisite to improving one's living conditions.

Privileges and lack of opportunity

Vicky is the founder of Escuela Nueva. She has also been the long-standing director of this programme, which translates as 'new school'. After an interview in her office, Vicky showed us Bogotá's picturesque outskirts and we had a chance to chat with her some more. Vicky remembers becoming aware of her privileged situation at a very early age. Fortunately for her, Vicky's family could afford to send her to a good school and provide her with a comfortable life in general.

As is common in some countries, Vicky finished her sociology studies in Bogotá at a young age. She began teaching educational sociology at different

---

12 Enrique Peñalosa was the mayor of Colombia from 1998 until 2001 and implemented measures which aimed to integrate the more impoverished parts of the city's population.

Colombian universities when she was barely 20. Even though she had a lot of fun trying to show the soon-to-be teachers how education can change a society, she soon became aware of the barriers against real change that existed within the academic system. While visiting a rural Colombian school – thanks to an invitation from the organisation, World Teachers – she became particularly aware of the academic challenges her country faced and grew to understand that the key problem for rural regions was education. If the quality of education could be improved here, the effects of this would surely have a positive impact on the quality of life for all Colombians.

Before Vicky truly dedicated herself to this project though – she knew that she would one day do this and was absolutely certain of that – she wanted to attain the necessary tools. She therefore decided to accept a scholarship at the prestigious Stanford University in Palo Alto near San Francisco. Over the two years Vicky spent there, she did her best to learn as much as possible about sociology and education. She declined several interesting job offers in the USA after graduation, and her peers and other acquaintances at the time could not understand why. Nevertheless, Vicky moved back home, realising that the potential for improvement in the Colombian educational system was more important by far.

Out in the countryside

Vicky accepted a position on the board of education after her return to Colombia. She had already developed a clear vision of her goal back in the USA. She wanted to tackle Colombia's greatest challenge, which was education in the country's rural regions. She spent weeks driving through the most remote areas of the country as she wanted to find out exactly where in these regions she needed to start. While driving through Colombia's rural regions, Vicky discovered schools in which first through to ninth graders were all taught in the same classroom. She learned that many children left these schools after just a few years because it was difficult for them to learn anything in these squalid and depressing classrooms.

The beginning of a new system: Escuela Nueva

Vicky spent two years with a highly motivated teacher from her team who came from a small rural school. They implemented a technique called 'try-out, remove and improve', a new didactic teaching method. Escuela Nueva, a systematically thought-out and financially effective concept, was the result of their work. Escuela Nueva's focal point was a cooperative teaching style which completely redefined the teacher's role. Teachers were no longer the only source of knowledge; instead they were seen as moderators for the learning process. This brought about changes in the curriculum, including new forms of teacher training and lesson plans. The children learned the subjects relevant to their everyday experience. They helped teach each other and furthered their own knowledge by asking one another questions. The children's confidence also grew – something that had not been seen in the classrooms before. Furthermore, the communities became more integrated as the children's projects spread beyond the classroom. The unification of different local stakeholders helped to develop a system that improved the quality of education at an affordable price. Every child could now receive an education – for only €3 a year.

Real results unify stakeholders

From the beginning, it was clear to Vicky that the new system would only have a chance if she produced documented results. From the very start, scholars specifically assigned this task were also part of the endeavour. But making changes within an existing school system is difficult anywhere in the world. During our interview, with a canny smile Vicky stated that her degrees in sociology helped her to build trust with the upper level of administration. The most important thing, however, was to support this trust with documented results. Thanks to the example of schools which were successfully implementing the model, along with the help of manuals and materials, this was not a problem. At the same time, Vicky also managed to get financial backup from international organisations. After nine years, the team had achieved its goal, and Vicky's changes became Colombia's new scholastic norm. Now 20,000 Colombian schools use this new system.

After earning political recognition and placing her work into the trusted hands of her colleagues, Vicky left the project behind for two years to focus on being a parent. Thereafter, as a result of her successful educational model, Vicky was appointed deputy of education and her solutions slowly gained international interest. The young mother received delegations from 30 countries which came to Colombia in the mid-1980s to learn about her success with the Colombian school system.

UNICEF – the new challenge

One day, Vicky received a surprising phone call from the United Nations Children's Fund's (UNICEF) director in New York, offering her a position as UNICEF director of education. Unfortunately, Vicky did not want to move to New York due to family reasons, so she declined this honourable position.

Alternatively, she accepted a position as director of UNICEF's Latin American and Caribbean offices as a regional educational adviser instead. With these titles, Vicky saw the opportunity to use UNICEF as a platform for expanding Escuela Nueva throughout Latin America in order to spread its positive impact on society. This would indeed happen in the years to come.

What was not working out as well as hoped, however, was the further expansion of the system in Colombia itself. Shortly after Vicky left the Department of Education, the entire government was re-organised. Latin America was taken with the idea of decentralisation and the good innovations which had been made in the past were lost along the way. Those with political responsibility wanted to immortalise themselves by implementing their own new models – regardless of how effective the older models had been. Unfortunately this re-organisation also affected Escuela Nueva and it was abandoned in many parts of Colombia. Fortunately, Vicky had founded the organisation, Escuela Nueva Volvamos a la Gente ('let us give the new school back to the people') before accepting her position at UNICEF. She was therefore able to further develop Escuela Nueva on a small scale and kept it alive in Colombia while working at UNICEF.

Refocusing

Although Vicky enjoyed her work at UNICEF, she decided to leave the organisation in 1997. She could not stand by while 'her baby', Escuela Nueva, slowly died. She went back to her roots and, with the help of a small team, started to rebuild once again. Luckily, her new marketing strategy had quick success, largely because Vicky could look back at Escuela Nueva's results from the last two decades. The positive energy associated with Escuela Nueva in the late 1980s also came back, and after a strenuous phase of reconstruction, Vicky once again had visitors from all over the world. She was even invited to present her model in international circles. Vicky stated to us that the reasons behind her success, aside from the actual work, can be easily explained:

> It is the same everywhere in the world: a good quality education is the foundation on which society is built. The problem is staring us right in the face when in Latin America alone, 60% of the population is illiterate.

Vicky tried to approach the reconstruction of Escuela Nueva with more business sense this time around. Previously, she had handed out all of her materials for free and had rarely conducted follow-up visits to see if her vision had been properly implemented. This led to different Escuela Nueva models throughout the world, some of which saw success and some of which did not. One benefit, though, was that the different models catered specifically to individual target groups and local communities.

The business model and franchising

Vicky faced several new challenges. In addition to developing teaching materials to fit new, interactive technologies, and tackling problems with quality on an international level, Vicky needed to find financial support for her model. Continuing to support and advise individual countries with which Vicky had contracts had its advantages, but it was not the right method for spreading Escuela Nueva throughout the world. She did her best to study the examples of former businessmen to understand what it would mean to develop a financially sound business model for Escuela Nueva. The World Economic Forum in Davos, which she had come to know through the Schwab Foundation in the last few years, helped her with this task. Together with the London School of Business, she developed a new type of franchising system. Vicky wants to use this franchising system to distribute Escuela Nueva along with certain products, such as teaching materials. Only the next few years will tell how successful this franchising system will be. After more than 30 years of developing Escuela Nueva, her main goal is to make the new model even more professional.

The programme, as it becomes more efficient both within and outside of Colombia, is partnering with more companies that can provide financial support. The honour of being named the Skoll Social Entrepreneur in 2007,[13] and the great financial contribution received as part of this award, will help with this next step. It will also help expand Escuela Nueva to 20 more countries. The Escuela Nueva conference in spring 2006, which 1,500 people attended in Medellin, shows that there is great interest in this new educational model. Medellin, once known for drugs, is today known for its art and will hopefully be known for education in the future. But the main goal is for education to once again become a priority in Colombia. In 2007, the Colombian government declared its plan to implement Escuela Nueva once again in its schools with the help of Vicky's team.

What really counts

With all the success and awards she has received in the past, and with all the remaining tasks and new challenges, Vicky told us there is one thing that shouldn't be forgotten. She said,

> The awards and distinctions, and being one of the 100 most important people in Colombia's history is good for gaining recognition and financial support. What really brings me peace, however, is that I have the opportunity to make school systems better. I have the chance to improve the education children receive in many

13 www.skollfoundation.org/grantees/a-e.asp

communities. I am able to watch as these young people change, as their confidence grows, and as they realise they have a chance to make something of themselves. I am motivated to get up in the morning because I know that there are positive changes being made for the children, and this is creating a peaceful atmosphere for those living in the communities. These are the moments that we work so hard for, regardless of what other people think.

Information

- www.volvamos.org
  Website of the Escuela Nueva foundation.

- www.schwabfound.org/schwabentrepreneurs.htm?schwabid=660
  Information about Vicky Colbert at the Schwab Foundation for Entrepreneurship.

- www.un.org/millenniumgoals/education.shtml
  Information concerning educational improvement, a goal of the millennium.

- www.pps.org/reference/epenalosa-2
  Organisation of Enrique Peñalosa.

'When you finish your life and you have a comment to make two minutes before you die – what are you going to say? You came and consumed in the sea of all this poverty? I want to leave a dent in the world, just a little impact. Because of my existence, I want the world to be a better place.'

Isaac Shongwe
Slum dweller, political
scientist and economist,
entrepreneur, philanthropist
Johannesburg, South Africa

Isaac Shongwe – A lost child of the slums and an African leader

'We can eradicate poverty and inequality if we work as hard for it as we are willing to work for big money,' said Isaac Shongwe when we met him in his South African home in the early part of 2005. Isaac knows what he is talking about. He was born in Alexandra, one of the worst black slums called 'townships' by the white elite, during the time of apartheid in Johannesburg. Isaac never knew his father. When he was ten, his mother died following a severe illness and he was left alone. This fate is far too common in Africa, and has become even more common since the AIDS pandemic began killing many young mothers and fathers who face financial difficulties. Their children continue to struggle on the verge of death in their parents' tin sheet homes, begging for their daily bread or earning it illegally. The situation for Isaac was not much better, 'I could have turned into one of the many street children,' he told us. Often, he did not know where his next meal would come from as nobody cared for him. Sometimes he even thought about ending his miserable life – nobody would have missed him. The world, he said pensively, should not be a place like that. Today, however, Isaac Shongwe is a successful businessman in Johannesburg and invests much of his energy and money in order to improve the situation of people who are forced to rely on support.

The wonder of education

By some miracle, there were people in Isaac's life who supported him, who gave him something to hold on to and hope for. One of these people so strongly believed in Isaac's talents that he gave him the possibility to continue his education after he reached the age of 12. This was most likely the decisive turning point in Isaac's life. As he told us during our interview, education changed his existence. 'I am one of the few lucky people who were given a chance. My chance was education. Today you can drop me anywhere in the world, and I will survive thanks to it.' Isaac took this chance very seriously. After he graduated from school with an excellent record in the early 1980s, he received a stipend to attend a university in Great Britain. Since he had experienced first-hand as a young man the desperate situation that the apartheid system created for 90% of non-whites, he wanted to learn as much as possible so that he could change this system. At first, he thought that politics was the right way to do this. So he made efforts to get another scholarship in the USA. However, after he arrived there he realised that politics was not quite for him and so he decided to simultaneously take up business studies. In 1987, Isaac graduated from the politics and business programme at Wesleyan University with honours and returned to his home in South Africa.

First steps in African business

First of all, Isaac wanted to prove himself. From 1988–1993 he worked for different enterprises, including Barloworld among others. During his free time, he graduated from a marketing programme at the Witwatersrand University in Johannesburg. In 1991, he was chosen for a Rhodes Scholarship for management training in Oxford, Great Britain. On his second return home in 1993, Isaac supported Monitor, a noted American consulting firm that hoped to begin business in South Africa. All of this was after the apartheid system had been abolished. However, says Isaac, it happened that customers refused to accept presentations given by a black South African. Only a few whites really believed blacks were capable of doing these things. Most believed that they had achieved their good positions due to new support for minorities. Because of experiences like this, Isaac also wanted his job to help spur the transformation process in South African society. This meant creating the same opportunities for the advancement of the 90% of the population who were not white.

Founding his first enterprises business

In order to promote the necessary changes more actively, Isaac founded his own consulting firm, Letsema Consulting. In this business, he applied himself to giving well-educated minorities a chance to work in high-quality jobs. According to Isaac, these people are predestined to bring about changes necessary for the country. In recent years, the state issued laws according to which all people should have equal opportunities for work. These laws also demand that disadvantaged minorities should have the opportunity to possess a certain percentage of company shares. In large corporations, such integration programmes for the non-white population are called 'black economic empowerment'. In many cases they are developed by Letsema.

Because Isaac quickly realised that it was not sufficient to produce studies and reports about necessary structural changes or to introduce training programmes for new employees, he founded Letsema Investments in 1998. With Letsema Investments, Isaac is seeking out blacks and people of colour who are reasonably able to implement a redistribution of property as prescribed by black economic empowerment programmes. Transactions are structured in such a way that 10–20% of a company's shares are transferred into the possession of well-educated, non-white South Africans. This way, property conditions in South Africa are hoped to gradually conform to the population structure – even though it is still a very long and arduous process.

Isaac himself holds shares in Barloworld Logistics Africa, and has assumed various executive positions. This is an opportunity to lead the way by example, showing what modern African enterprises could be designed like in the future, and how they might better integrate the population so that the country's inequalities are mitigated.

Satisfaction through a high-flying career and money?

It is a fascinating success story – 'the orphan from the slums fights his way up to become a financially strong multi-entrepreneur.' Even more extraordinary is the other side of Isaac Shongwe. All in all, said Isaac, his enterprises were a way of becoming financially independent and enabling him to do what he really wanted to do. He explained that it was his goal to have enough money by the age of 40 to be able to dedicate himself completely to social projects. Isaac was always clear about the fact that he did not want to become a normal capitalist:

> When you finish your life and you have a comment to make two minutes before you die – what are you going to say? You came and consumed in the sea of all this poverty? I want to leave a dent in the world, just a little impact. Because of my existence, I want the world to be a better place.

He did not want to fade away and forget his childhood. He did not want to repress anything. Rather, he wanted to remember how thankful he could be that others had supported him. As soon as he founded Letsema Consulting, at a stage in which most other people would have prioritised their own well-being, Isaac created the Letsema Foundation. He supports educational projects in order to give as many other people as possible the chance that he had, by providing stipends and other models of support.

For years now, the young entrepreneur has spent between 30% and 50% of his time on projects that lead to more equal opportunities for people and, this way, are aimed at reducing poverty. He calls himself a social entrepreneur, a social capitalist, convinced that social justice in South Africa can bring about many positive impulses for successful businesses. Early on, he was honest and courageous enough to know that all the money he earned would not make him happy, or as he expressed it to us when we met him: 'You can go and have the most expensive dinner, but if you have it by yourself it loses its purpose.'

Challenge for responsible leaders

As time went by, Isaac became more and more aware of the support that existed for entrepreneurs such as himself, who implemented their own values in business; life sets an important course for the positive development of Africa. So in the years 1998 and 1999, Isaac started regular conversations over breakfast with other young, successful entrepreneurs. At the meetings he always challenged them, asking whether they wanted to become 'regular capitalists' – as can be found all around the world – or whether, with consideration for the history of their country, they wanted to become capitalists of a new stripe. By visiting the townships with them and organising other activities that brought the country's inequalities right before their eyes, he made it clear that people in positions of leadership have enormous responsibility for the weaker members of society. Within a short time, Isaac's group expanded to 100 managers and together they began organising social projects.

The right idea at the right time

At that moment, in fact just at the right time, Peter Reiling from the Aspen Institute[14] gave Isaac an inspiration. Peter, having been the executive director of the successful development organisation TechnoServe[15] for many years, suggested training the next generation of African executives with the help of an African Leadership Initiative.

This idea was exactly what Isaac was looking for:

> Money is easy. We know how to make it, but our main game is to change the world. We need community-spirited, value-based, ethically-motivated leadership. Let's build the bridges! We have to create a new economy. It is certainly important what you do with your money. But it is also important how you earn it.

As Isaac told us, for him it was never really an option to accumulate money without reflecting on what he would do with it. He thinks his soul would have shrivelled if he had thought like that. Again and again he emphasised: 'To be a real leader means that you show in leadership how you can serve your society.'

14 The Aspen Institute is a think-tank with the mission of fostering enlightened leaders and an open dialogue. With seminars, conferences and initiatives in leadership development, the institute supports independent research and the appreciation of timeless values. Leading personalities from the spheres of international politics, economics, art and sciences are invited to join a regular exchange of ideas.
15 TechnoServe, business solutions for poverty in rural regions, is a non-profit organisation which supports people with an entrepreneurial spirit in developing countries. It provides them with the same professional consulting that otherwise is used by leading, international businesses.

Casting out the money-hungry

Isaac did not hesitate. He committed himself to lead the 'African Leadership Initiative' to success on the African continent. It is his aim to create a network of leaders who dedicate themselves to the real problems in the world instead of focusing only on themselves and their own interests. According to him, society must ostracise entrepreneurs who only act in their own interest. 'We have to create a culture, a movement that isolates and shames such people.' Isaac thinks that only those who strive for a better world and earn their money in 'win-win-win-situations', meaning profit for themselves, for society and for the environment, deserve the respect of their fellow human beings.

A holiday home? A vineyard? A yacht?

Isaac's own experience told him that selling one's soul for money is tempting, especially for well-educated, intelligent, capitalist-minded black Africans. If you ask Isaac what his motivation is under these circumstances, he will answer with conviction: 'Life is not about money. Money is good, but it will not make you happy.' During our interview, he continued with passion, 'You buy a holiday home in Cape Town, and then you realise you can buy a vineyard and you can buy a yacht . . . how much is enough?' Everyone has to answer this question for himself. Isaac knows from his own experience that capitalism can 'suck you in' very quickly and financial success can get you hooked on having more and more. Nevertheless, he decided for himself that he does not want to waste the chance that was given to him because another person believed in him.

Economic activism in boardrooms

Isaac wants to create a like-minded community of what he calls the 'socially creative'. If they have the right positions in government, economy and civil society, these people can have a positive effect on the world, which is not to be underestimated. He is convinced that we can eliminate poverty on earth if more and more people share this attitude and way of thinking. Day by day, he works to mobilise human capital and send it to where the supply is still running low – to the business of improving the world. He likes talking about what he calls 'economic activism', and we asked ourselves whether his remarks only hold for South Africa or perhaps have certain validity across the borders:

> You look at how the apartheid system was defeated. It was defeated
> because some of us who grew up in a township were activists. We

were so convinced that the system was wrong, we were prepared to die for it. That activism is gone. My strong feeling is that we need to bring back that activism. But now, because we are a democracy, it needs to be in different areas. There is a new enemy out there! Those of us who moved out of the townships don't see that enemy. However, one of the things that keeps me awake at night is the huge inequality that exists. So I organised some meetings with the young leaders from the African Leadership Initiative in the townships. And now they are doing community projects there. We have the responsibility and perhaps even the possibility for the first time in history to defeat this enemy.

Information

- www.africanleadershipacademy.org
- www.letsema.co.za
  Website of the company founded by Isaac.
- www.aspeninstitute.org/leadership-programs/henry-crown-fellowship-program
  About the Aspen Institute's Henry Crown Fellowship Programme.

'With the help of art I am trying to show people how the way we live is connected to certain effects on the environment. I want to provoke them to reconsider certain habits.'

Mia Hanak
Art history major,
environmentalist, traveller,
entrepreneur
San Francisco, USA

Mia Hanak – Why mobile phones earn a place in museums

Mia Hanak, barely 30 years of age when we met in one of the small and trendy restaurants on one of the many hills of San Francisco, explained:

> The environmental movement has been very 'in your face', showing mass destruction, deforestation, the oil spills and all that and people are numb to it. They don't want to see it, they don't want to be a part of it and – worst of all – they don't want to contribute to it. In very few cases has it actually created more awareness about how things are connected to each other on our planet. I travelled through over 40 countries when I was younger. I lived with the people of Kenya for over half a year. I made my way through the jungles of Mexico and Guatemala. I was struck by the beauty of the glaciers in northern Argentina and the remainder of the rainforests in Madagascar. But everywhere I went, I saw the same sad picture. Our growth-driven society leaves its trace even in the last corner of the planet, and often destroys these wonderful natural refuges. These dramatic moments in nature showed me early in my life that we don't have a lot of time to spare. We have to do something; many of us have to do something – right away.

However, there is no use in constant panic, she said. The focus should be on putting positive and long-term solutions in place.

Founding the Natural World Museum

Mia's professional background is in neither travel nor environmental science. Coming from a family with an affinity for art, she decided to study art history and anthropology, later pursuing a master's degree in museum management and exhibition design at the Tufts-University in Boston, and consequently becoming involved with American museums for the first time. Following her extensive travels, however, Mia saw the necessity to dedicate herself to protecting the environment. Since she is not a woman of words but of deeds, she decided in 2001 to find an innovative combination between her compassion for nature and her love for the world of art. Together with the art collector Richard V. Smith, a mentor and supporter, she founded the Natural World Museum (NWM) in San Francisco.

At the beginning, the project was not quite a museum, but rather a kind of travel exhibit concerned with environmental topics. Thanks to Smith, who had bought a very large collection by Robert Bateman, one of the best known wildlife artists and environmental proponents worldwide, it was easier for Mia to organise the first exhibitions:

With the help of art I am trying to show people how the way we live is connected to certain effects on the environment. I want to provoke them to reconsider certain habits. At the Natural World Museum we want to inspire people by organising exhibitions at the highest level of art that leave a strong impression with the viewer. Currently we are also the long-term ongoing partner for the United Nations Environment Programme (UNEP). We have exhibitions here in San Francisco, but also internationally. For instance, we will have a permanent installation in Nairobi, Kenya, at the UNEP headquarters. Also, in 2008, we are planning on producing the major environmental art expo for the Beijing Olympics. For these occasions, we have artists working with us from all over the world.

Although it sounded as if her project had been spoiled by success, Mia faced many issues early on and had to take several brave steps to prevent chances which offered themselves along the way from escaping.

Four months that meant the world

One such step for Mia was when the World Environment Day of the UNEP came to San Francisco in 2005. Mia sneaked into one of the meetings of those politically responsible for the day. She used all her persuasive skills to get the mayor to commission her and the Natural World Museum with the organisation of a large exhibit for World Environment Day. When the mayor surprisingly agreed, she rejoiced, but only for a short time. As soon as Mia's thoughts cleared up, she noticed the scale of the task she had just presented herself with: the whole world would have its eyes on San Francisco that day. There would be thousands of visitors, including very influential people who would come to see the city and exhibition. Finally, however, she composed herself and thought that, actually, this was perfect, except the whole event was only four months away.

After an incredible effort of thousands of hours and thanks to the formidable work of her team, the impossible became reality just in time: The largest environmental exhibition worldwide was staged under the title 'Urban Jungle'. With quality standards as high as a museum, the exhibition received attention from politicians, environmentalists, the art scene and even Hollywood stars. The work of photographers, sculptors and multimedia artists, matched to the main topic of the conference, demonstrated the beauty of nature in the context of modern cities. From around the world, 100 mayors also saw the exhibit and were similarly inspired to push environmental topics with the same dedication that they had seen in San Francisco.

Why mobile phones destroy the homes of gorillas and create violence

Mia's favourite topics are the complex cycles and dependences of today's world. Her work illuminates how seemingly unconnected phenomena, such as gorillas and mobile phones, are linked to one another. One of the exhibits in the Natural World Museum explains how coltan, a mineral used in mobile phones, is excavated at the cost of sacrificing the wonderful forests of Rwanda, the habitat of the gorilla. At the same time, the mining of this precious mineral triggers violence and corruption in Rwanda and other countries of West Africa. Finally, the metal is used as a component of mobile phones and quickly ends up in our rubbish bins. On the other hand, Mia loves the almost picturesque nature paintings of Robert Bateman. His breathtaking work stands for what the Natural World Museum wants to convey with its art: a powerful message of beauty and hope about our environment, instead of threats and apocalyptic impressions.

Hot with a thermos

At our meeting, Mia smiled and ordered a glass of wine. She did not want to eat anything. When she has the chance, she likes cooking for herself – something light and healthy. Overall, her lifestyle has changed. In the land of huge cars, she uses public transport, wears environmentally friendly clothes, uses resource-intensive commodities as economically as possible, and has replaced soft drinks in plastic containers with a thermos filled with tea. But there is no sign of eco-blandness. She is an attractive woman enjoying life to the full. She is just determined and is setting a living example of the values she wants to convey to others: 'It just makes sense to think about alternatives, you know. And there are so many possibilities. The sky is the limit when it comes to innovations in the environmental sector!'

The Olympic Games, books and more

As we watched Mia and listened to her, we had no doubt that she wants to produce bigger results. 'Slow down? I don't see it coming before the Olympics 2008. Even my family likes my involvement. But they think that I'm crazy and ask themselves when I'll ever find time to get married.' Next, she will publish a book about environmental art[16] and perhaps another one about her travels

16 The book was published in July 2007 under the title, *Art in Action: Nature, Creativity and Our Collective Future*. The Natural World Museum was closed after organising a number of exhibits. Mia's new venture is Millennium Art.

to over 40 countries. Mia's actual vision is to organise art exhibits that can be replicated in museums all over the world. We don't find it hard to believe that we will see this happening in the future. In the end, connecting art with the environment has been part of Mia's upbringing, during which she painted over the adverts on the back of her mother's shopping trolley. Who would have thought that this young girl would grow up to become an art historian and renowned manager of environmental art exhibitions around the globe?

Not only sunshine

Certainly, success does not come for free. Mia confessed to us that working long nights and weekends without end was leaving a trace. Even though the exhaustion in her eyes was covered by her smile, she admitted:

> Of course, the work I am doing requires a certain conviction. From first day one, I worked for about US$100 a week. That is not just a job, it's a passion. But I can't imagine anything more rewarding. Money is just not an option at the moment. I am motivated by people who believe in a common goal.

Information

- www.millenniumart.org

  Mia's new venture that, along with a number of others, designed the CO₂ cube at the COP15 in Copenhagen.

CONCLUSION

The following represents five insights and experiences from Chapter 2:

1. All age groups have their unique virtues and challenges when it comes to creating a positive impact. All of them are appropriate

2. Young people excel at action, innovation and courage; older people bring in valuable networks and a healthy distance. Fields of work can change over time

3. Doing something meaningful is a great way to rejuvenate

4. The journey is the destination. Learn, experiment and build on what you experience

5. Not the scope of impact is what counts, especially at first, but the fact that you take off on the journey will give you plenty of satisfaction and meaning

3
'I'm not financially secure'

The saying goes, 'Money can't buy happiness'. Ultimately this statement drives towards the question of how much a person needs to live, when 'enough' is truly 'enough'. And the answer is often by far less than is generally assumed. When we told friends and acquaintances about our travels after our return, we often heard the reaction:

> That's all very interesting – but for me it wouldn't work. At the end of the day I have to live on something, pay for my apartment and my car. In order to get involved and make positive change I'd have to earn enough. In the end, it seems the whole thing is only for rich people.

When we then told them about some of the people we had met on our journey, such as Karen Tse or Florian Krämer, who had set off on this path without any financial means to speak of, but 'only' with determination, a first idea and a great deal of passion, we mostly received sceptical looks and glances of disbelief. Admittedly both of these people do not drive the newest cars, nor do they know the latest fashion trends. But they are happy in their work every day and know why they are here on earth.

The more we describe the deep satisfaction and joy in living that we witnessed in our interviewees, the greater the interest and curiosity of our listeners. Doing good and becoming happy doesn't require an overflowing bank account. The stories in this chapter show that one can live successfully and be fulfilled without great financial reserves.

'My vision gave me the necessary inner strength. I wouldn't have been able to do anything else because I would have felt like a dead person walking if I had renounced my life calling.'

Mariana Galarza
Holistic doctor, cook book
author, seminar leader, family
entrepreneur
Quito, Ecuador

Mariana Galarza – Promoting health instead of curing illness

Mariana Galarza picked us up with a Land Rover in the 2.5 million-person metropolis of Quito at the beginning of 2006. The capital city of Ecuador lies on an elevated plateau, 2,400 metres above sea level. One hour east of Quito, she manoeuvred us through steeply descending streets to the tiny city of Pivo. Born in 1950, Mariana grew up here as one of 11 children. It was thanks to the extraordinary strengths and abilities of her mother, who became a widow early and only remarried very much later, that she and all of her ten siblings went on to college, Mariana told us. Her mother managed to reconcile her family duties with the establishment of her own textile business, all the while ensuring that none of her children felt deprived.

In Pivo, which lies in the heart of a beautiful mountain terrain, Mariana developed a love for nature and people. During the drive she told us about her childhood dream of becoming a doctor. Beginning in her early years, she would read the exciting life stories of great doctors and imagine their selfless work for the service of humanity. She saw their careers as a struggle for good and the health of all.

A difficult beginning

This made the shock all the greater when Mariana had to submit to the reality of medical school in Quito. During her eight years of study, and then a further two of specialisation in alternative medicine, she had to overcome crisis time and again. She could not accept that medicine cared exclusively for people who were already sick, and that these people often were only dispensed high doses of medication: 'In the hospital they care for illnesses, not for people,' Mariana said. In her experience it was rare that doctors would take the time to understand the lives of the people whom they treated. Often she had the feeling that the doctors did not even heal people long term, but instead created dependences on medications and the next medical examination. It was always about the short-term treatment of symptoms, about a pill here and a vaccine there.

Mariana had chosen her career out of genuine idealism, not in order to make sick people somewhat less sick for a time. Her goal was to heal people long term and above all to help healthy people stay healthy. Because she came from the country, she was inspired by traditional medicine based on natural, active ingredients, which she had admired in her youth. Even today, only about one-third of the Ecuadorian population has access to medical services. The majority, however, know how to help themselves with plant substances and a well-balanced diet. This medical knowledge was passed down in Ecuador from generation to generation and is now experiencing greater esteem again. Among the main elements of this knowledge are the principles of cold and warm food and spices taken according to one's health condition, along with that of a deep respect for nature and its balance and for the values of the community.

Yet Mariana was also conscious that traditional medicine and idealism alone could achieve no credibility in our modern society. So she struggled successfully through her study of medicine and gathered experience in academic medicine in order to gain financial freedom and independence. She remarked, 'You need idealism, but you also need knowledge!'

Money as a life goal versus childhood ideals

Since she did not like working in hospitals, after finishing medical school Mariana opened a private practice in one of the affluent districts of Quito. Business-wise things were going well for her, but she realised very quickly that her life calling did not lie in helping rich patients. Along with her private practice, she opened a health centre in her home town Pivo. She wanted to overturn the usual paradigm of medicine that existed there by serving poor people first and foremost. She did not only want to heal sick people, but also to make it possible for healthy people to obtain preventive care so that they could remain healthy. To achieve this, Mariana founded the Asociación Vivir (which means Life Association in English) in 1987 in order to translate her childhood ideal of holistic medicine into reality. She gave advice on exercise, the meaning of nutrition and traditional healing methods, which often offered the best solutions for local illnesses.

In the beginning Mariana's patients were not happy with her holistic approach. Pleased to have a modern doctor among them, they demanded medications, but they were less enthusiastic as the young doctor explained to them that merely taking pills would not lead to long-term health. If they wanted to be really healthy and stay that way, they had to change some of their personal habits and consciously make health a goal in their lives.

Holistic and long-term health

The first health course that Mariana led in Pivo was only attended by five, good female friends. However she didn't allow herself to be discouraged. She explained to us over a cup of tea:

> My vision gave me the necessary inner strength. I wouldn't have been able to do anything else because I would have felt like a dead person walking if I had renounced my life calling. I believe that

each of us has a mission in this world. We are not here just to be
born, to live and to die.

Mariana continued to study, worked in her city practice for financial reasons, made contacts and daily grew better at communicating her ideas to others. She had the feeling that her vision gave her the creativity to find more new ways to get closer to her goal. Over the years, she completed a diverse continuing education in alternative medicine, herbal medicine and healthy cooking which helped her to consolidate herself as a specialist in a broad range of health maintenance topic areas.

A beautiful massage room for rich and poor

Over time, her patients – who could barely afford expensive medicine – learned to appreciate Mariana's work more and more. So, over a period of nearly 20 years, her health centre went from its humble beginnings as a small health station to a multi-complex with large buildings surrounded by gardens. We viewed the property, and in one of the waiting rooms we discovered a cook book published by Mariana with tips on healthy cuisine. In one of the other rooms there were rows of neatly marked pharmaceutical bottles in which Mariana stored herbs and other remedies. In one other building, we were surprised to find a calm, aesthetically pleasing massage room.

We had rarely seen such a thing in a medical facility, and never in a developing country before. Wellness and atmosphere are an important component of health, Mariana explained – that is true for poor people as much as it is for the rich. She added: 'I don't work with the poor, I work with people. You meet all kinds of people everywhere. Some are nice, some are unfriendly. Some are helpful, and still others possess more or less money.' The rich pay somewhat more for the services of the centre, the poor less, but all of them receive the same attention and care.

In recent years the Ecuadorian government became aware of Mariana's work. This led to a constitutional recognition of the native Ecuadorians' medical knowledge in 1998. Today Mariana's Asociación Vivir has begun health projects in 19 of the 22 provinces of Ecuador. For example, in six provinces a large-scale study is being carried out on how malaria cases can be reduced with the help of the knowledge of the natives. In this study, different components from the Vivir knowledge base are united. The mix of healthy nutrition, preventive herbs and a well-balanced lifestyle are supposed to strengthen red blood cells, the condition of which has a great impact on malaria risk and above all on the outbreak intensity of the illness. Moreover, the natives in the Amazon region are knowledgeable about several healing plants and edibles that strengthen the immune system and can be used with great success for certain illnesses. Their methods are especially helpful in the case of illnesses and epidemics with high fever, to which malaria belongs. Principally, this knowledge targets prevention first and foremost: that means, through its application, the spread of a malaria infection into an epidemic can be prevented. The suspenseful question is whether a significant decrease in malaria can be achieved in these regions in the next five years.

Not only healing illness, but cultivating health

Through her organisation, Mariana tries to broadly implement a paradigm shift towards health-supporting lifestyles and habits that have been promoted by many doctors for years. She pleads again and again for concentrating on the cultivation of health instead of purely on the cure of acute illnesses. Many believe this to be the right attitude for a developing country because hardly any customer can pay for expensive medications. Yet even in industrial countries, enormous sums of money could be saved if doctors would ingrain this attitude in their patients more strongly than before. The money saved is, however, only one side effect. The quality of life of many people would be improved in leaps and bounds if they took preventive care of their health.

Increasingly, Mariana works directly with businesses and communities. With businesses she develops health programmes and gives seminars on holistic, healthy living which include the specifics of implementing healthy working conditions. These programmes initially have positive effects on individual workers who implement her advice into their daily lives. In the longer term, the business also benefits as the health – and with it the efficiency – of workers is improved across the board.

The team, now 14 in total, offers similar services to communities. More and more often, whole 'Celebrations of Health' are organised in order to celebrate in style the progress of people who have changed their habits. With all of these activities, Mariana wants to reach the point at which people change themselves and begin to understand that they can, in a large part, fashion their own lives and health. In truth it is her goal – though it might sound somewhat paradoxical – to make the work of doctors mostly superfluous.

Keeping the family together

Through the years Mariana has also learned a great deal about entrepreneurship and efficient business practices. In her organisation she relies only partially on donations. The various consultation assignments are one source of income, and she wants to develop another with her husband, who has supported the work of her organisation for years. They want to produce organic food products to increase the health of people even more. The money earned will flow into the work of Vivir. Her daughter also helps out. When we met her, she wanted to study public relations and then assist in the organisation. Mariana was pleased about this, and also had an explanation for the involvement of her family:

> It is simpler and better to work with an ideal in mind. It allows you to learn, to study and also to suffer a little bit. Having an ideal also helps to keep the family together. That's not a theory – it's our reality.

Information

- www.avivir.org
  Website of Asociación Vivir.

- www.ashoka.org/fellows
  Mariana was an Ashoka Fellow in 2005.

'Every morning when I see the children, I know that I'm doing the right thing.'

Florian Krämer
Adventure traveller, African
aficionado, social scientist,
blessing for AIDS orphans
Kapstadt, South Africa

Florian Krämer – Children deserve a better world

The Lake Constance region, situated in a triangle between Germany, Switzerland and Austria, is a beautiful area. Fruit orchards lie picturesquely on the fertile shore of the lake; in the background, the Austrian and Swiss Alps rise slowly upward, creating a peaceful, country idyll. In this region, one of the warmest in Germany, Florian Krämer spent a happy and carefree childhood. Driven by curiosity about the great wide world and – as he mentions in conversation with us during the early part of 2005 – the usual naivety of a 19 year old, he and a friend looked forward to an adventure of a particular kind together. After their secondary school graduation, they planned to fly to Zaire (which today is the Democratic Republic of Congo), and from there begin a long trek to South Africa. It was a dream they had held for a long time and now they wanted to put it into action. As they boarded flight AZ 394 in the beginning of April 1994 both were full of anticipation. Neither of them had any idea that their dream trip would transform into the greatest nightmare of their lives. Only a few days after beginning their trip, Florian Krämer's experience of Africa would go on to determine the course of the coming years.

The end of naivety – the war

Without having informed themselves very well about the escalation of the political situation in this central African region, Florian and his friend were unmercifully taken by surprise. Shortly after their arrival they witnessed the most terrible civil war that Africa has ever experienced. During our meeting, Florian does not want to describe in detail yet again what they encountered there, since it pains him too greatly even more than a decade later. Anyone, however, who knows that more than four million people lost their lives in this war can guess without the need for words what the two friends had to experience as they attempted to make their way north through the Republic of Congo in order to flee.

Most of the borders to the majority of the neighbouring countries had been closed so, together with other refugees, the two friends marched as if in a trance around 600 kilometres across the country in order to reach the one still traversable border of Uganda. Indescribable scenes and barely endurable suffering paved the recent graduates' route each day. As they reached the mountains north of Goma, nearly collapsing from exhaustion after days on end of marching, Florian simply could not go any further and remained behind, lying exhausted in a mountain forest, fully aware that these could be his last minutes. But, as Florian told us, the courage, tenacity and altruism of a nine-year-old indigenous boy saved their lives. He found them in the forest at night, took Florian by the hand, and pulled him along until he followed the boy in a daze. After several hours, the boy simply left the two friends in front of a house and disappeared once again into the forest. To his astonishment, Florian learned over the course of the next few minutes that an English ambassador's family, who were stationed in Uganda, lived in the house. For the time being, Florian and his friend were rescued and the war fire was only distantly audible over the next few days.

Weakened by the difficulties of their flight to escape, the two young men both became infected with dengue fever. Almost as though he were experiencing it all over again, Florian told us how they attempted to get medication from the local hospital while running high fevers. However, as they saw the many people who were maimed by the war, the suffering from AIDS in the corridors and the crying children – who during the last few days had become orphans – Florian was almost ashamed to ask for medication for his fever. This situation of indescribable suffering was, for him, the moment in which he swore to himself to devote his life to the children in Africa – if he should get through all of this alive. Florian Krämer was certain on that day in the hospital that he could transform these tragic experiences into something positive, into something positive for the many children of Africa.

Fulfilling the promise

When we interviewed him, 11 years had passed since these traumatic experiences had occurred so, we wondered, what had become of his vow? According to Florian, at that time he managed to finish the trip through Africa in order to gain other impressions of the continent. Afterwards, returning to Germany did not come into question for him. He had the feeling that he had found the right place to turn his unspoken promise into actual deeds. In memory of the many orphans in Zaire and Uganda, he wanted to build a home for HIV/AIDS orphans and decided to begin studying social sciences in Kapstadt. From there he began to take long trips around the continent in order to become more familiar with the countries and their people and learn first-hand about the lives they faced. During this time he also had many very beautiful moments, which were, however, interrupted again and again by the often sad realities of African life. During the semester holidays, Florian often worked in social services. In this way he spent much time with disabled and abused children and was the leader of a school for street children. In all of these projects he learned more and more about the catastrophic situation of many children in Africa.

Childhood and AIDS in Africa

Besides the daily problems of getting clean water to drink and food to eat, hygiene conditions and lack of education were the greatest problems for many children in the poor districts. It hit those hardest who became orphans because of the spread of HIV and who were left in a daily struggle for survival without any kind of support. The number of these children is growing each year, possibly because many African governments tried to deny and hush up the AIDS problem for a long time. For a country such as South Africa it is hardly possible to overlook the consequences of this terrible illness. In the year 2004, the rate of infection was assumed to be around 21% in the population of 15–49 year olds. It was subsequently estimated that beginning in 2008, 500,000 people would die annually from this disease. For this reason, between 1990 and 2005 the life expectancy was reduced by 22 years, from 65 to 43 years of age.

More than anyone else, the many children of AIDS patients suffer the devastating consequences of the disease. Often fathers leave their families and the mothers – sick or overwhelmed by the situation – leave the children to themselves. When there are no nurturers at all, the children have to take care of themselves. Every hour, 16 children in South Africa become orphans; some of them are already infected with HIV themselves. All of these experiences confirmed and strengthened Florian Krämer's decision to build a home for AIDS orphans.

The first steps – and disappointment

So, with great energy, he began this project after completing his studies in 2002. He wouldn't allow his young age to stand as an excuse to begin later. Yet how do you establish an orphanage directly after graduation without financial means of any kind? Since Florian had just enough money at that time for a flight back to Germany, he organised slide show presentations with the help of friends, relatives and acquaintances at home. At these he reported on his experiences in Africa and his dream to build a home for AIDS orphans. After one year of hard work and many presentations, he had convinced and inspired enough people with his plans. He managed to collect enough money to return to South Africa and begin building a home.

As Florian told us at the interview, when he looks back, it was the right decision to follow his heart and begin his life project directly after graduation. Many people wait, he said, until they have collected enough experience, skills and money, but often by that time it is too late for them. They are afraid to incur new risks and to put the comforts of the lifestyle that they have earned on the line.

Good will and money don't have much influence in Africa

However, as Florian Krämer returned to South Africa with the urge to work, goodwill and €50,000, he learned that the government had decreed a ban on building new orphanages. Behind the decree was the thought that only a small number of children should grow up in institutions. More than that, the South African government wanted to obligate the extended families to care for orphaned children, as had always been the custom. This approach was not actually a bad one, however it was simply not feasible due to the enormous number of orphans, Florian explained.

Florian wouldn't admit defeat that quickly, so at the beginning of 2004, he began to search for an existing project which he could support with his work as well as his donation money. For a long time, his search was futile and he was close to giving up.

The light at the end of the tunnel

But then he came across a day-care centre in Nyanga, one of the largest poor districts, 20 minutes outside of Kapstadt. His hopes were not actually very high as he made an appointment with Muriel, the founder and leader. To begin with, the trip was more like adventure travel than a normal commute. No white person had had the heart to travel into the disreputable township for months. There were as few paved streets as there were street names and house numbers. As he finally arrived, 60-year-old Muriel and her husband, who had founded the day-care centre 15 years ago, received him warmly. Even after the first few minutes it was clear that Florian had found people here who were on his wavelength. Muriel's centre was but hours away from closure. Financial means for further licensing were lacking. But that could not discourage Florian. He had big plans. On the empty lot next door he already envisioned his new orphanage taking shape. And that's how it happened, too.

A stranger and a blessing

Since then, time has flown for Florian. Sharing tasks with Muriel is working out well. His responsibilities are organisational and business-related matters, while Muriel takes care of all the educational aspects. In the first two years of his job, Florian not only put the day-care centre on a solid financial footing with the help of the donated money, he also doubled the number of places available, founded a pre-school and made preparations for the next expansion.

In the beginning, Florian had concerns about how the people in the township would react to him. He is still the only white person who comes here every day to work. However, up until now he has remained unmolested, although shootings and violence are on the daily agenda all around the nursery, and rival gangs also use firing squads to ensure the hierarchy in the district. Probably by now the secret rules of the slum protect him. The natives have given him the nickname 'Yentsikelelo', which means something like 'blessing' in the local language Xhosa.

A progress report: highs and lows in South Africa

As we began writing the manuscript for this book back in Europe, we received the following progress report from Florian:

> When Muriel Hollow, the co-director and original founder of the project, was granted the neighbouring lot by the city in 2000, there were unending difficulties. An old building with many garages is located on the lot. The building belongs to the city of Kapstadt, but is occupied by some area inhabitants. They run illegal bars there. They store the alcohol in the garages. Besides that, parties are held there and more or less legal business is transacted there. The police occasionally raid the garages and find stolen cars.
>
> Since 2000, Muriel has been fighting to have the building vacated, as it now belongs to our property according to contract. Since 2004, I have also been working for this goal, but unfortunately with little success. Endless discussions with the public authorities have led to nothing. Our legal entitlement to the building is not being questioned; however, the legal situation doesn't help you much in this area. Nepotism and corruption among the authorities make the matter even more difficult.
>
> In March 2005, we received a large donation to be used for building a new day-care centre. This was housed until that time in an old metal shed. After some weeks of construction – two external walls were already complete – two of the squatters came into our project and threatened to destroy the new building if we did not arrange for the immediate end of construction. Since we did not back down before this threat, they destroyed the two newly built external walls after continuing heated debates which involved the whole community.
>
> Why do the members of a community destroy something that is being built for them and their children? The niece of one of the perpetrators even works in our nursery. Our workers stood there with tears in their eyes, and the children of the school looked on the ruins of their new building, stunned. They had watched the building grow daily and waited on its completion full of anticipation. Of course we did not initially have any more money for rebuilding, and since the metal shed was not there anymore, the day-care

children had to play outdoors throughout the whole winter. But despite the many difficulties, we didn't give up. In January of 2006 we again had some capital and were able finally to complete the building in August of 2006, without further incident.

Shortly after the destruction of the building, a much greater personal trial was imposed on me. One afternoon in August 2005, I was threatened with a pistol at an intersection while I was in my car on the way to work and just barely came away with my life. My car and everything that was in it were stolen, of course. I was fortunately able, however, to escape in the last moment, which in robberies of this kind is usually impossible. The fate of three other white men at the same place, who were attacked and shot directly next to their cars in full daylight, shows just how impossible. I was asked the next day, whether I would stop with my work. Although I was still in profound shock, the answer came within seconds: Under no circumstances!

I still don't know even today, one-and-a-half years later, where I took this conviction from in that moment, but it came from deep within my heart. I had not thought for even one minute about giving up. Not because I'm stronger than others, and not because I have no fear of a new attack, not because I believe that I have a special guardian angel or that I am untouchable. Rather simply because my work is much more than a job. It is a life calling. It challenges me and brings me to the borders of self-awareness. It makes me stronger. It rocks me between great strength and despair. It fills me with the firm belief that our daily achievements in this sometimes comfortless ghetto are not just a drop in the ocean. In other words, it is a daily gift. And I could never say out of conviction that my children deserve to be abandoned just because two poor, desperate young men threatened and robbed me. I don't know how long I can push my luck. But as long as I have the strength to continue this work and as long as I feel that my work has an effect – that's how long I am prepared to make every sacrifice for this life calling.

In the meantime, I have also realised that it does not make sense to be angry at the perpetrators. I experience every day here how broken homes, poverty, violence, alcohol, unemployment and abuse drive many young people into indescribable desperation. Desperation, out of which there is no visible escape. All of this is a consequence of the brutal apartheid policies, the white population of South Africa's instrument of control.

I came to the realisation that I cannot do anything else but forgive these two young people for their crimes. And I already understand that this forgiveness is not even a generous gesture on my side, but simply a human necessity, if we want to break out of the endless circle of violence and hate. And whenever I experience daily how much poverty, AIDS and criminality has reduced the value of a human life in South Africa, I become ever more conscious of how grateful I can be that I did not only survive, but that I am also allowed to continue to do this work!

Information

- www.indawo-yentsikelelo.org
  Website of Florian Krämer's organisation.

- en.wikipedia.org/wiki/HIV/AIDS_in_Africa
  Background information about the topic of AIDS in Africa.

'It's my duty to improve my own existence, but also the existence of the people around me.'

Njogu Kahare
Agricultural scientist, tree
planter, inventor, co-worker of
a Nobel Peace Laureate
Nairobi, Kenya

Njogu Kahare – Live your own values

Many people have heard the name Wangari Maathai[†] before – she was the first African woman awarded the Nobel Peace Prize in 2004 for developing the Kenyan environmental organisation, the Green Belt Movement (GBM). Her comrades-in-arms were, however, as interesting as she and, although they have not won any Nobel prizes themselves, they worked behind the scenes and helped to shape the organisation's success with their dedication and motivation.

In Nairobi we spoke with Njogu Kahare. We met with him under an old, dignified-seeming palm tree in the fragrant garden of the organisation head-quarters in 2005, a setting fitting for the work of the GBM. Njogu Kahare was a fascinating presence; one eyelid hung down slightly due to an infection, hiding the majority of his left eye and giving him a somewhat secretive expression. His personality was marked by humility. Njogu was 40 years old and the father of four children when we met him. He had been with Wangari Maathai for almost 20 years – and not all of these years were as full of glory as those following the Nobel Prize. His story begins in Nyandarua, a village in the west of Kenya. We had an idyllic image of rural Kenya in mind: green savannah, wild animals waiting for safari tourists and picturesque little towns with colourfully dressed, smiling people. But this is only a part of the reality. Another part is the unbelievably quickly growing desert. The portion of the land that is useful for agriculture is growing smaller and smaller, but must feed more and more people. Intense cultivation and deforestation are endangering the people's living environment and leading to conflicts and flight. These are some reasons for the bitter poverty that still reigns in many areas of Kenya – exactly as in Njogu's home town.

All beginnings are difficult

'It was my childhood dream to move to the capital one day,' Njogu recalled. The dream came true when he moved to Nairobi to study agricultural science and was able to graduate in 1989 after four financially difficult years. After that, he hoped to improve the agricultural situation in his country through a job as a government officer, and to earn enough money to bring his wife and his first son to the city. However even as Njogu looked for a position, the Kenyan government implemented a hiring freeze. He had to return to his home town, where the living conditions were very hard. Together with his wife and son, he lived in one small room and tried to earn at least a necessary minimum wage by raising trout.

One day, friends from the city visited him and subsequently told a certain Professor Wangari Maathai about Njogu's experiments with farming fish. The scientist, who was the first Kenyan woman to receive a doctorate and who taught at the University of Nairobi, invited Njogu to speak with her in the city. Her reforestation project, the GBM, was still very small and Njogu had never heard anything about it. The two got into a deep conversation over several hours. Although Njogu found Wangari Maathai's work very exciting, he returned to his role of fish farming, which offered him at least a minimum of financial security. The intellectual exchange preoccupied him, however, and so he went by the GBM office during one of his next trips to Nairobi.

The power of a good memory for names

Even at our interview, he still clearly remembered that particular morning:

> It was still very early and the gates were closed. However, I could hear the sound of a typewriter. Astonished that someone was already working so early, I tried to look through the window to recognise who it was. I was surprised as I heard the voice of Professor Maathai calling my name. After all, we had only met once half a year before.

In the following intense discussion, Njogu let himself be persuaded to take the risk and begin building up new alliances and tree nurseries in his home region for Professor Maathai and the GBM. After some months, Njogu realised to his joy that he had found in the GBM an organisation in which he felt comfortable. Here he was able to achieve a positive contribution for others and fully live out his potential and creativity. This outweighed by far the initially deplorable pay and the strong hostility he was confronted with in his daily work.

Having to justify offering support

Namely, most people in the country were sceptical when Njogu tried to explain why it was good for them to plant trees. They suspected that he would charge money for the support that the GBM offered. For many it was hard to believe that there might be people who simply do good things for others, without profiting from them financially. Njogu's difficulties increased as the Kenyan intelligence agency turned its attention towards him and attempted to intimidate him. Since Wangari Maathai had begun to advocate against several environmentally damaging projects, the GBM was seen as an anti-government group.

> In 1993, when the GBM was nearly considered an enemy of the state, we had to change meeting locations often and sometimes organise secret meetings because of the government persecution.

Professor Maathai was imprisoned three times. But each time public pressure helped free her again.

The many meanings of the trees

Despite all of these difficulties, in only two years Njogu successfully established 94 tree nurseries and groups to care for them. These groups are wholly ecological and economic assistance projects. First and foremost it is women who join forces and receive GBM seedlings, which they then plant and care for on their own, or on school or churchyard, soil. Through this, they gain wood for their cooking ovens, are able to plant vegetables in the shade of the trees and earn their own income through the sale of the vegetable harvest and new seedlings. An income immensely improves the position of the often still strongly disadvantaged women in the society. Long term, the GBM would like to sensitise people to the environment and offer them solutions that make sustainable development possible. The GBM aims to counter the over-use of natural resources through which farmers are destroying their livelihoods and are forced to yield giant acreages to the spreading desert, as in the north of Kenya. In many parts of Africa this is leading to incredible suffering.

From fieldwork to office work

In February 1993, Njogu suffered a bad retinal infection. At our meeting he speculated that the illness was caused by the many bicycle trips he took from community to community on dusty tracks. Even when we met, his sight was limited due to the infection. Because of his illness, he was afraid that he would lose his work at the GBM, which he had learned to love. Instead he received an offer to oversee improvement of methods and workflow from the headquarters in Nairobi. Above all, this meant creating an environment in which university graduates could be hired and motivated to stay. In 1991, Njogu was actually the first and only university graduate at the GBM, but he successfully reached this goal and by 2006, 15 academics worked for the GBM. Many of them were working on the optimisation of quality control for the 6,000 tree nurseries. By now, ten partially international programmes have been established that are constantly being further developed.

Njogu was now happy that a government job didn't work out for him:

> Very early on I understood that, in order to survive, I either had to use dirty tactics, which most people use in the established system – and which would kill my creativity – or I had to play a completely different game. I didn't want to work in a culture in which people didn't want to share their ideas because someone might steal them.

I didn't want to work in a culture in which people exclusively follow their own best interest rather than the greater good. The GBM gave me the option of playing a completely different game and preserving my creativity and values.

Build 100 dams immediately

Sometimes Njogu missed the fieldwork. But then he recalled the happy eyes of people when they proudly presented their own trees or a small income. With especially fond memories, he thought back on a programme which built small dams for irrigation:

> In 2003, we built an embankment dam for a village. As we finished and watched the water flow in, we looked to the women of the village. They stood there and were simply happy that they didn't have to walk hours anymore to fetch water for cooking, or for their animals and trees. Such an experience gives you an incredibly deep satisfaction and motivation. You feel as if you should build 100 more dams right then and there. It doesn't matter how much strength it takes.

Even in the everyday routine of the office, such memories retain their power.

The family's incomprehension

As a consequence of his work, he could proudly show his four children the many trees and dams he had been responsible for in the last decades. However, Njogu also thought back on the difficult times, when his own family treated him with incomprehension and almost disrespect. They did not understand why a university graduate would prefer a job with an anti-government organisation to a well-paid government post. In the beginning, Njogu had no financial security and most of his relatives predicted a miserable end for him at the GBM. Yet when he looked back on the intense, deeply personal engagement of the GBM workers over the last years, it did not surprise Njogu that they have achieved what the world now admires them for.

The prize of prizes and the meaning of values

Njogu found it fitting that the public awareness of the GBM has significantly changed thanks to the change of government in Kenya in 2002 and the Nobel Peace Prize given to Wangari Maathai in 2004. However, he also saw the dark side of this sometimes overwhelming public interest. Many greedy and ego-tistical people became interested in the GBM after 2004, and it became diffi-cult to distinguish the well-meaning supporters from the people who wanted to be involved for self-interested reasons. In spite of this, the team has not had difficulty in making the right decisions thanks to the organisation's deep-rooted values. Njogu said with certainty:

> There is nothing more important than values – that's what I have learned. Values such as self-respect, self-reliance, volunteer activ-ity, belief in oneself and the necessity of paying attention to the small, crucial matters that bring the big ideas into motion – those are the cornerstones of the Green Belt Movement.

Over the decades, Njogu and the whole GBM team have modelled these values for people in Kenya and have spoken again and again about respon-sibility, transparency, community empowerment and the power of a few well-intentioned individuals. After Wangari Maathai won the Nobel Prize, all this turned around to benefit the organisation. Njogu almost rhapsodised when he said that he sometimes couldn't believe his own luck at being a part of the GBM:

> It is my duty to not only improve my own existence, but also the existence of the people around me. It's a pretty ambitious goal, because so many people don't even know what direction they want to go in or what improvement means in the first place. When you work for the Green Belt Movement, you have to think about those things.

Information

- www.greenbeltmovement.org
  Website of the Green Belt Movement.

- www.nobelprize.org/nobel_prizes/peace/laureates/2004/maathai-bio.html
  Biography of Wangari Maathai[†] for the Nobel Peace Prize award ceremony.

- Maathai, W. (2010) *Replenishing the Earth: Spiritual Values for Healing Ourselves and the World* (New York: Doubleday).

- Maathai, W. (2010) *The Challenge for Africa* (New York: Anchor Books).

- Maathai, W. (2007) *Unbowed: A Memoir* (New York: Anchor Books).

- Maathai, W. (2004) *The Green Belt Movement: Sharing the Approach and the Experience* (New York: Lantern Books).

'It's not the destination, it's the journey. And it's not what you are able to do on the outside. But it's who you become in the process of working towards your dream.'

Karen Tse
Attorney, Taoist, bundle of
energy, human-rights warrior
Geneva, Switzerland

Karen Tse – The journey is the destination

When we met at the beginning of 2005, Karen Tse summarised her experiences of the last few years with a mix of sceptical despair and calm assurance:

> I can remember moments when I would just sit on my couch and cry; I was so depressed because I couldn't see the end. I would ask myself, why in the world am I doing this? In Cambodia the police officers know nothing about gathering evidence. Whoever they grab gets tortured until they confess. The police stick them in prison and consider the case closed. What keeps me motivated is the improvement of such seemingly inescapable circumstances.

Her organisation, headquartered in Geneva, is called International Bridges to Justice (IBJ). Karen has been involved for years in the implementation of legal standards in criminal trials. She initially set her focus on Cambodia, China and Vietnam, but her long-term goal is to train criminal defence lawyers in more and more countries so that no one will be tortured or held prisoner without a trial.

From California to Cambodia

Karen Tse is a young woman of Chinese-American descent. She completed her law degree at the University of California, Los Angeles (UCLA) in 1990 and then worked as a human rights lawyer and public defender in the USA, primarily in San Francisco. In 1994, she went to Cambodia in order to help with the reconstruction of the public legal system which was completely destroyed by the Khmer Rouge. For three years she worked on behalf of both the Judicial Mentor Programme of the United Nations Centre for Human Rights and the Cambodian Defender Project in the country, which had not yet recovered from the terrible reign of the dictator Pol Pot and his army. Among other things, she was responsible for training criminal defence lawyers – when she arrived, there were only three of them in the whole country. This work left behind deep traces. Once, Karen visited a 12-year-old child who had been tortured in prison. His offence was attempting to steal a bicycle. The child suffered from continuous fear every new day because he had no idea what ordeals might be in store for him. Actually, the child was entitled to a public defender. But instead, a confession was tortured out of him simply because those working in the judicial system were historically accustomed to doing so.

Laws that no one knows

Karen explained to us that countries such as Cambodia do not in any way reject human rights. Quite the opposite: many of them have a very modern criminal law code. But the course of justice viewed as self-evident in Western countries has yet to really take root in this region – culturally as well as in professional training. Often, knowledge needed for evidence gathering or professional questioning of witnesses is lacking. Sometimes simple tools such as recording devices, cameras or computers are unavailable.

In close cooperation with the government, Karen and her colleagues have conducted countless seminars for criminal defence lawyers and people who are involved in the justice system in order to make adherence to the new laws possible. They have also informed the population about the rights of defendants and delinquents, so that the applicable law has at least a chance of being implemented.

Theology as the next step

After her return from Cambodia, Karen decided to study at the Harvard Divinity School, a non-denominational university for theology and religious studies, and become a priest. Her religion, Taoism, fascinated her and she wanted to find her continuing path in it. Yet the experiences in Asia would not let her rest. So, in 1999, still during her studies, Karen wrote a strategic plan for improving the criminal justice system and its implementation through the help of an organisation, first in Cambodia, Vietnam and China, then worldwide. Karen remembered this time:

> I was completely naive when I started IBJ; I had no idea how hard it would be. I really, really did not. I saw the gap in the system and I realised it was not being met. So I thought that I was going to start this project: I had this great idea that everybody in the whole world would come and help me, I would be finished with it in a year – having created the organisation – and I would move on with the rest of my life.

Idealistic naivety and money

This idea turned out to be mistaken in the months that followed. Because her husband's work required him to transfer, Karen moved to Geneva. Soon her apartment was occupied daily by voluntary helpers. There were no full-time paid workers because donors were scarcely found in this early stage of the organisation's development and no one was willing to work full time for

IBJ for free. And yet Karen worked hard and continuously with her changing team of volunteers, in order to implement as many of her solutions as possible even without money. It took two years before the many exertions were rewarded with the first larger donations.

For Karen it was a difficult and depressing time. But her organisation was no normal business idea which you could simply scrap if it brought in no money. IBJ filled a gap, a need that wasn't being met by anything else. 'Someone had to take care of these people,' she said, 'why not me?'

Karen is an energetic, happy person. As soon as she starts talking, you are overwhelmed by her passion and warmth. The strength that she has leaves an immediate impression. She learned to see the difficult times as a kind of test. It helped a lot that the financial upkeep for her family was secure through her husband and his work. For the organisation and her own career there were no guarantees – she had to carry that risk herself.

The rights of the accused

Today, IBJ has a comfortably decorated, permanently busy office. The small team organises seminars for criminal defence lawyers in cooperation with the local governments in its focus countries of China, Cambodia and Vietnam. Along with that, information campaigns are run in order to enlighten the population about its rights, and mentor partnerships are offered between Western and Asian criminal defence lawyers. In China, for example, in 16 provinces a Campaign for the Rights of the Accused was carried out in cooperation with the national legal aid centre in the languages of Mandarin, Mongolian, Tibetan, Uyghur and English. At country-wide training conferences, hundreds of criminal defence lawyers and public defenders were trained. In addition, the first Chinese handbook for criminal defence lawyers, a guide to all existing legal and trial regulations as well as their application, was developed and distributed. IBJ also helped develop a web platform on which local criminal defence lawyers and legal aid centres can inform themselves about existing regulations and the latest developments.

As some of our interview partners – who work for the worldwide, active network of social entrepreneurs and have watched Karen's work closely for many years – have recognised, all of these activities and Karen's cooperative approach have done a lot of very positive things for the human rights situation of people in respective countries. Some of them even think that her work has achieved more than all of the many delegations of large international organisations and governments have done. Similar results are also being targeted in Cambodia and Vietnam, and the public interest in the work of IBJ has been growing thanks to the good results. Organisations such as the Skoll Foundation, which can provide the possibility of financial support, have also found their way to this small, but effective group.

Criminal defence lawyers, educate yourselves and multiply!

When Karen looks into the future now, she sees countless possibilities for raising the quality of life of many people on the planet through an improved implementation of the existing criminal justice laws. Since she can now rely on financial support, her plans are realised ever more quickly. As the next big step, the establishment of an International Defender's Institute is planned in order to satisfy the inquiries from many countries needing help with the development of structures for a fair and effective criminal justice system. IBJ plans to familiarise a group of criminal defence lawyers from these countries with the rules of modern criminal processes in intensive courses. In this way they will be put into the position of being able to subsequently implement the model in their own countries. They can act at home almost as drivers for change, and train thousands of lawyers as criminal defenders. The institute will make it possible for criminal defence lawyers from around the world to use the infrastructure and technical knowledge of IBJ. In addition, an international fellowship programme is being developed so that the efforts to create international partnerships can be strengthened.

The journey as destination

When Karen looks back on her not always simple time at IBJ from today's perspective, she is deeply satisfied with the outcomes that she was able to achieve with her team, in spite of it all. Of course we wanted to know whether she regretted choosing this journey at any point, whether she had ever really thought about giving up. To that she responded:

> More and more I realise that, in the beginning, I was only very goal-oriented. But finally, I changed my attitude and I realised two things: Number one, you have to decide, it's not the destination, it's the journey. And it's not what you are able to do on the outside. But it's who you become in the process of working towards your dream.

Only over the course of time did she understand why each day left her with a feeling of satisfaction, in spite of all its difficulties: she was a part of a solution, not a part of the problem.

Programming happiness

Karen is convinced that people can only become happy when, instead of thinking selfishly about their own well-being, they manage to connect their life to a higher goal that is bigger than them. In order to do that, it is of course not always necessary to begin a new initiative. Everyone can use his or her skills to contribute to something larger, even a computer programmer, Karen suggested dryly.

> He doesn't have to develop a war game or bank software the whole day. He might, for example, program a multimedia training course for criminal defence lawyers or an information management system for the 2,500 legal aid centres in China.

Only a few years ago, Karen would hardly have dreamed that she would one day lead an organisation in which she influences the lives of so many people daily. Had she not listened to her inner voice in the first two founding years of IBJ, many more people would be helplessly suffering torture in the legal system. Although there is still much to be done worldwide in this area, the work of IBJ brings hope and confidence to a few countries on the planet. Karen allowed herself a poetic moment and a serious expression came over her usually smiling face:

> Khalil Gibran said, 'Your joy is your sorrow unmasked. And the self-same well from which your laughter rises was oftentimes filled with your tears.' So joy often comes out of exactly the same deep places that suffering comes from. I am thankful for the challenges that I experienced while building up IBJ.

Information

- www.ibj.org
  Website of International Bridges to Justice.

CONCLUSION

Here we present you with seven major insights and experiences from Chapter 3:

1. The financial situation is very relative and subjective to a person's needs and, especially, perception

2. For some people the issue of material rewards becomes very secondary over time, once they do what they love to do. Others find ways to reconcile financial and other needs. Look out for smart set-ups, models and combinations

3. In any case, it is immensely helpful to be aware of your financial needs, especially compared to other life priorities

4. When you start an own venture, you believe in your vision and work intensively towards it, you will very likely find financial support. During the planning and start-up phase, however, you should be patient for two to five years. Often this will mean adjusting your lifestyle, working a second job simultaneously, or finding people who support you

5. Your new venture should enable you to create structures that are reliable and have relationships with project partners that are stable. In the case your project fails, your new clients must not find themselves stuck in great difficulties

6. If you decide to work as an employee of a company, you can look for a work area where you can produce a positive impact from within, such as a social intrapreneur

7. During the transition and new orientation phase, the support of family and friends is a great asset

PHOTO IMPRESSIONS OF OUR WORLD TOUR

PHOTO 1 The entrepreneurs of one of farming projects supported by Development Alternatives (DA), close to the Indian city of Jhansi (see the portrait of Ashok Khosla on page 143).

PHOTO 2 The village of Punawli, the location of one of Development Alternatives (DA)'s 'TARAhaat' internet cafés.

PHOTO 3 The production of hand-made paper from cotton scrap in one of Development Alternatives (DA)'s training centres.

PHOTO 4 A women learns to produce bricks in a Development Alternatives (DA) training centre.

PHOTO 5 The millionaire and philanthropist David Bussau with one of his projects in Barangay Silangan, Quezon City, Philippines (see the portrait on page 127).

PHOTO 6 Safia Minney at the opening of the 'Whole Foods' markets in London, selling organic and fair-trade products in the city centre (see the portrait on page 25).

PHOTO 7 The office of People Tree in Tokyo.

PHOTO 8 One of People Tree's stores in Tokyo.

PHOTO 9 Karen Tse with Cambodian prisoners (see the portrait on page 101).

PHOTO 10 The authors with Roma Debabrata and one of her daughters (see the portrait on page 167).

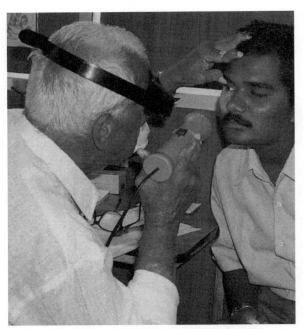

PHOTO 11 The 80-year-old Dr V examining a patient at the Aravind eye clinic in Madurai in the south of India (see the portrait on page 51).

PHOTO 12 Dr Aravind Srinivasan, ophthalmologist, economist and Dr V's nephew.

PHOTO 13 Checking material delivered to Albina Ruiz's garbage collection system (see the portrait on page 19).

PHOTO 14 Albina Ruiz (centre) receiving her prize from the Skoll Foundation, presented by the foundation's director Sally Osberg, founder Jeff Skoll (right) and actors Robert Redford and Ben Kingsley.

PHOTO 15 Refuse collectors working with Albina Ruiz's garbage collection system.

PHOTO 16 Chris Eyre with his wife and grandchildren – one of the great motivators of his charitable engagement.

PHOTO 17 Florian Krämer with children in his day nursery in the Nyanga Township close to Cape Town (see the portrait on page 87).

PHOTO 18 Children and young women from Florian Krämer's project during a singing and dancing performance at the Waldorf school in Überlingen, Lake Constance.

PHOTO 19 Jordan Kassalow examining a patient (see the portrait on page 157).

PHOTO 20 Finally being able to read again – thanks to glasses from Scojo Foundation.

PHOTO 21 The Argentinian choreographer Inés Sanguinetti, during a performance of 'The Nobodies' in Hamburg, 2004, together with artists from the slums of Buenos Aires (see the portrait on page 135).

PHOTO 22
Youth in Buenos
Aires engaged
in one of Inés
Sanguinetti's
projects.

PHOTO 23 Mia Hanak with children of Nairobi (see the portrait on page 73).

PHOTO 24 Mia Hanak at UNEP in Nairobi with Nobel Peace Prize winner Wangari Maathai (second from the left) and the former director of UNEP Klaus Töpfer (right), inside the installation 'Trapped Inside' by the Natural World Museum.

PHOTO 25 Wolfgang Hafenmayer interviewing Njogu Kahare (see the portrait on page 95).

PHOTO 26 Njogu Kahare's nursery and 'laboratory' of the Green Belt Movement.

PHOTO 27
Enthusiastic
students in one
of Vicky Colbert's
Escuela Nueva
schools.

PHOTO 28 Vicky Colbert (centre) receiving her prize from the Skoll Foundation, presented by the foundation's director Sally Osberg, founder Jeff Skoll (right), Nobel Peace Prize winner Professor Muhammad Yunus (see page 219) and musician Peter Gabriel.

PHOTO 29 Erin Ganju in the classroom of one of Room to Read's 300 schools (see the portrait on page 151).

PHOTO 30 Erin Ganju with a student of a Room to Read project.

PHOTO 31 The authors in front of the ruins of Machu Pichu in Peru.

4

'I am already successful with what I'm doing'

Why do people strike out on a new professional path, develop themselves in a new direction, or take on the risk of a new beginning? The reasons for such decisions are many and depend on each person's life situation. For outsiders, close friends and family, however, the motives such people take for setting out on a new path are sometimes less understandable.

In the following pages you will meet men and women about whom many of us would ask the question: Why would this person bother with making a change to his or her life? Based on the measure of success our society usually applies, these individuals had achieved almost everything that most people only dream of: financial success, a position of responsibility and recognised social standing, and power and influence. They were once multimillionaires or successful in their careers in business, art or entertainment. They occupied high-ranking offices or enjoyed the glory of standing on great world stages. Yet at some point in the course of their careers, they realised that what they had achieved wasn't really what they were looking for.

What is success?

If one defines success as 'the accomplishment of an aim or purpose', [17] *our interview partners can absolutely be characterised as successful people. They had reached many goals in their professional lives. However, in a sobering process they came to realise that they hadn't really thought about whether these goals also coincided with their personal goals. Would these professional goals lead to increased satisfaction and happiness for themselves?*

[17] *Oxford Online Dictionary*

This painful question led to a change of heart. From then on, our interview partners thought carefully about which professional goals would also satisfy their individual passions and values. And they tried to recognise what they would like to look back on later in life with joy and gratification.

'If you are poor, you have no choices. You are economically disempowered. I want to help enable people to choose. That is crucial for a person's development.'

David Bussau
Orphan, millionaire, founder
of the investment company
Maranatha Trust, investor in
social enterprises
Sydney, Australia

David Bussau – The economy of 'enough'

As a child, David was left by his mother in front of a boys' home in New Zealand. An online profile reads,

> He left the orphanage at the age of 15, opened a hot-dog stand at the age of 17, and was a multimillionaire at the age of 35, growing and managing an extremely successful contracting business in Sydney.

After recounting David's life, most journalists lapse into paeans of admiration. He seems to embody the fascinating 'rags to riches' mythology. The way the story goes seems predictable: years of success, one innovative business idea followed by another and rocketing profits for a hero slowly turning grey. However, David Bussau's life doesn't quite fit this scheme.

It was for this reason, that the management consultancy Ernst & Young nominated him as the Australian entrepreneur of the year in 2003. The laudation mentions that making money proved to be an empty promise and, when a cyclone devastated the city of Darwin in Australia, the storm steered David's life in a whole different direction: In 1974 David responded to an SOS call from an Australian town ravaged by a cyclone. He put together a team to help rebuild what the cyclone had destroyed. Afterwards, in 1975 he founded a private non-profit trust through which 12 global organisations have been established to address social issues.

David is the founder and visionary behind Opportunity International Australia, an organisation credited with revolutionising aid given to support social expansion through the principles of micro-enterprise development. It now creates a new job every 35 seconds in 27 countries. David continues his work by building relationships and consulting with governments, international businesses and other organisations that share his vision and join the fight against poverty and degradation. That is a short and factual résumé of a millionaire distinguished from 'average' millionaires by a lifetime filled with surprising turns.

At home with a bare-footed millionaire

Prior to our interview, we wondered, 'what is at the core of a man with a biography like David's?', and set out to walk in his footsteps. Towards the end of 2005, we arrived at a modest, but comfortable-looking house situated in a quiet suburb of Sydney. We were invited into a living room with somewhat old-fashioned furnishings. A fresh and content looking man in his early 60s sat across from us. As is fitting for an Australian, he wore shorts, a sporty polo shirt and no shoes. He exuded a sense of tranquillity, ease and inner peace of mind. His eyes were lively and now and again we had the impression of a mischievous twinkle in them. Right at the beginning, David made it very clear that his motivation comes from his relationship with God: 'My sense is that the creator expects a return on his investment. He's invested a lot in me and I've been blessed because of that, so I've got to convert that investment into creating new, societal impacts.' David hesitated; he seemed to expect objections when describing the religious foundation of his life. He talked about God as a matter of course, as if he were a good friend sitting next door. There was no trace of religious fanaticism in the air.

No parents – no pressure

David's reflections on his life revealed some surprising insights. 'The best gift the creator gave me was to grow up without parents.' He explained,

> I can say this with all sincerity: I had to decide who I was myself. Most people are an extension of their parents, their parents shape them and their parents mould them. A lot of people I meet are messed up because of their parents. I never had anybody expecting me to become a lawyer or a doctor. And when I made mistakes, I had nobody to pay the bills.

David discovered who he was – all on his own. He learned at lightning speed how to make money and increase it. He lost a few fingers at work when he was 14 years old. The compensation he received from his employer's insurance served as start-up money for his first hot-dog stand. Suddenly he was the boss of his colleagues: he employed them to run other hot-dog stands. He learned all he needed for commercial success through private studies, which he often did early in the morning or late at night. He didn't have enough money for expensive universities in the beginning and later, when he did, he didn't have any time for them. The hot-dog stands had showed him that he had a talent for business. After that, his plans in life were easily made: 'I wanted to be a football star, I wanted to be wealthy, I wanted girlfriends and all that comes with it. My dreams were not that different from most teenagers.'

At the age of 30, David had already made a lot of money – tons of money, in fact. He had successfully founded several enterprises, run them and sold them. Lacking a financial network and family support, this was no child's play. But these years of deprivation were followed by years of abundance. Initially, David enjoyed the success and recognition. He had a challenging job and founded new businesses, the investment possibilities became more and more exciting and there were hardly any budget restrictions. But, was all this appropriate for David?

At the age of 35, David sensed that perhaps his life didn't suit him completely. At the time, he was the owner and director of a successful construction company in Sydney and was a partner or shareholder in 30 other businesses. In the early 1970s, Kerry Packer, who was then Australia's richest man, was giving a party at his mansion in Sydney. He suddenly realised that one door on a cocktail cabinet which David's company had installed was not closing properly. Packer called David up directly and demanded he come by immediately to fix the problem. It wasn't a good time for David, especially since he was in the middle of spending an evening with his family. On leaving his family, David was able to solve the client's problem without delay, but the situation made him think: 'I was so indignant that this person had power over me and could dictate to me: "You leave your kids, you come across and you fix the catch on my door".' The business and the money that he wanted to earn were the only reasons that he had to leave his family that night:

> That triggered something in my mind. Just because this guy owes me the money, do I have to change my whole values and fix the catch on this door? And that got me thinking: how much more wealth do I need? Is accumulating more wealth worth putting up with all this?

It wasn't the first time that such thoughts had come up, but it was the first time they had weighed on him so heavily. Many conversations with his wife followed. These talks revolved around values, goals, and the Christian faith, to which David had for years granted little importance. Finally his family decided they had reached the point which David calls the 'economy of enough'. He simply had enough money and earning more just didn't make sense.

However, this wasn't 'enough' for David in the sense of 'now I'm going to enjoy my wealth on a beautiful island', but rather the realisation that he could not become more satisfied through yet more money. He wanted to discover a deeper meaning in life and give something back to society. What exactly that meant was not clear to David back then. He only knew that he didn't want to continue as before. David's values, anchored in the Christian faith, helped him to make the following decision: over the next five years David started selling his shares in several enterprises and placed his growing cash funds in a family-owned trust cooperation. David's business partners met his decision with total incomprehension, but their views no longer interested him.

A life mission

David began the search for a life mission in Darwin once a cyclone had destroyed the north Australian city in 1974. He gathered together a number of colleagues and his family, they relocated for several months and helped rebuild the almost totally destroyed city. Owing to his experience in Darwin, David's help was requested after a catastrophe in Indonesia. It was at this time he decided to take on this new challenge together with his family:

> I spent five years in an Indonesian village, repaired bridges, lived with the farmers and helped them build houses and water fountains. That gave me some time to think about who I was, who I wanted to be and what impact I could make.

With time, he came to realise that the people who lived in the village remained poor despite all their efforts. His discontentment grew because he couldn't change anything about their situation. The specific attention he had directed to construction problems seemed wasted.

The power of micro-entrepreneurs

One day David lent US$50 to a farmer who wanted to buy himself a sewing machine. The farmer wanted to start a trade as a tailor. As soon as he could, he repaid David the money. This experience brought David back into a field he was familiar with: entrepreneurship. He quickly realised the power that lay in the support of micro-entrepreneurs. After five years of reflection and active searching, it seemed he had found the right path for himself. No one was better suited than him to support other entrepreneurs and show them a path out of poverty.

> Football was my dream, but it is not what I was created for. Today, my satisfaction comes from relationships, from seeing people flourish and develop, so that they can be the people they were created to be and can develop for the benefit of society.

Gifts and talent

When David talked to us about his convictions, his eyes gleamed,

> It is our purpose in life to be true to the gifts and talents the creator gave us. I was given the gift to be an entrepreneur and to know how to make money. I can now use this gift for the benefit of supporting those in need.

In the last 30 years, David and his constantly growing number of staff have helped about three million people build a better life. In the year of 1979, he founded the organisation, Opportunity International, together with the American businessman, Al Whittaker. Their common goal was to help people in unfortunate circumstances solve their own problems. The tool was money, small sums, but enough for small loans and basic training. In the 1980s, similar systems were launched worldwide and the economist Muhammad Yunus from Bangladesh became the most prominent representative of the micro-finance movement.

Opportunity International is an actively growing organisation. When we met David, the number of Opportunity International's clients in 28 countries was approaching one million, and the intention was to reach two million clients by the end of 2010. That amounts to sustaining millions of lives, since each entrepreneur can help many individuals climb out of poverty.

The value of good advice

David withdrew from Opportunity International and went on to support new organisations that are dedicated to fighting poverty. As an entrepreneur, he relies on the capitalist economic model. David never donates money; he invests it and expects financial independence. Today he is a shareholder in about 20 businesses which all share the goal of improving the quality of life of the poor. His advice and guidance are the most valuable gifts he can give and are much more important than money. David even passes on his experience to governments and NGOs. He is internationally active as a consultant, speaker and business coach.

David has never regretted dropping out of the business world nor retrying old formulas of success. He also does not regret the long period he spent searching for his true vocation in life. David is grateful that he has been lucky enough to have found a job in which he can make full use of his abilities and which gives his life meaning, 'If you are poor, you have no choices. You are economically disempowered. I want to help enable people to choose. That is crucial for a person's development.'

Over the years, David let go of the idea of wanting to leave something behind – whether it is a material or immaterial legacy.

> I came to this world with nothing and I will exit this world with nothing. I was given the gift of business sense. I mean, I never earned this gift; it just was given to me. The gift doesn't belong to me, so the fruits of this gift don't belong to me either. So, for me it's important to be a good steward.

Information

- www.opportunity.org
  Opportunity International USA.

- www.opportunity.org.au
  Opportunity International Australia.

- www.grameen-info.org
  Website of the Grameen-Bank of Nobel Peace Prize laureate Muhammad Yunus.

- www.oikocredit.org
  One of the world's largest refinancing parties in the micro-loan sector.

- Robinson, M.S. (2000) *The Microfinance Revolution: Sustainable Finance for the Poor* (Washington, DC, USA: World Bank Publications).

- Yunus, M. (2003) *Banker to the Poor: Micro-lending and the Battle against World Poverty* (USA: Public Affairs).

'No revolution without joy,
no joy without revolution.'

Inés Sanguinetti
Dancer, choreographer,
sociologist, social entrepreneur
for art and community
development
Buenos Aires, Argentina

Inés Sanguinetti – The wake-up call: uniting passions

'I am committed to movement; anyone devoted to theatre is committed to passion, tension and movement.' When Inés said these words at our interview with her in early 2006, we felt her vitality. We felt a powerful energy, her passion and yearning for movement. In Inés's life everything is about movement and passion – as a dancer, as a choreographer, and as a pioneer on the frontier between art and social development.

A family heritage of class oppositions

Inés Sanguinetti's mother is from the Argentinian bourgeoisie, her father from a classic, middle-class family. As a child, Inés experienced the social divide in Argentina inside her own family. Very often, the country's political problems would be controversially discussed while sitting at the kitchen table. The exclusion of whole sections of society from active life was an especially prominent topic. This was certainly one of the main reasons for Inés to study sociology in Buenos Aires and get involved in different social projects concerned with the people in the poor districts of the city, the so-called 'villas'. The growing inequality in Argentinian society and the sometimes extreme violence connected with it – especially where the poor, outcast and hopeless lived – made her voluntary involvement more and more difficult, however. When the first of her friends died in this situation, the young woman decided to leave this world completely behind her and concentrate on her second passion, modern dance.

In the following years, Inés perfected her dance style, worked in several modern dance ensembles, participated in international dance festivals and developed into a recognised choreographer. Day and night, she worked hard on her artistic career, which her family strongly supported. As Inés realised in hindsight, she had often felt lonely at that time. But her increasing success still gave her a feeling of satisfaction, 'I was developing my international career. At last I was proving the point that I could do it: I was very enthusiastic about all the good theatres and going to very prestigious international festivals around the world.' Even as the social inequality of Argentinian society and accordingly the poverty, hopelessness and violence grew worse from year to year, Inés no longer wanted to spend time on this aspect of her country. 'I had left it for dance. It was like a very big brick wall between my political past and my new life in the arts,' she recalled.

'My husband had to wake me up'

Her husband, Juan Peña, asked her just during this time of success: 'Is that your life? While Argentina is falling apart, you are dancing for the empire?' Inés could not and, in the beginning, did not want to understand him, and only replied: 'You know nothing about the arts, so just shut up.' And yet her husband's question did not leave her untouched. Juan showed her his answer. He gave up his prestigious job as a high-level manager at a large bank because he wanted to have more to look back on at the end of his life than his material wealth, a fast sports car and a much-too-large house. He wanted to have an assurance that he had made positive changes for others during his life. Inés noticed that, since he had established the foundation El Otro ('The Other'), he had begun teaching philosophy again on the side and was educating himself more broadly, he was much happier with himself and his life, even though he was no longer invited to elegant parties nor had important business decisions to make.

The path into the villas

Her husband noticed that he had triggered something in Inés and he stoked the fire:

> You were always interested in changing the world. Why don't you do something in your daily life for that? If the arts are so important for society, why don't you go and offer your modern dance in one of the poor quarters?

Provoked and motivated by these remarks, Inés went back into the poor districts of Buenos Aires for the first time in years. She was hesitant, felt awkward and uncertain about how relevant her art would be in this place in which people struggled through daily survival. But she was determined to move and to change things – with passion. 'The exciting part of interaction is, that it is always a movement,' Inés explained. As Inés began to visit people in the villas and to talk with them about art, creativity and dance, it quickly became clear to all that art really could help people cope with their difficult daily lives.

During this initial period, a group of 15 former drug addicts and violent criminals contacted Inés. These youths had begun a new life thanks to the work of her husband and El Otro, and now they were trying to bring other youths in the poor districts onto a better path. The group asked whether it would be possible for the choreographer to write and perform a theatre piece with them with their own life stories as its topic. It would be a kind of therapy play for the group and at the same time give others the courage to dare to take the leap into a better life themselves. Inés gladly took this invitation, never guessing that it would shape the next decades of her life.

Social exclusion is brutal

While working with the youth group, Inés realised how much energy, passion and creativity was hidden in these young people. Thrilled by the first results, Inés wanted to make it possible for the youths to perform their play outside of the slums. However, she quickly recognised what being a social outcast truly means. There was hardly a stage outside of the poor district that would allow them to perform. Even the youths were afraid to leave the slums. They feared not to be accepted by other Argentinians for their skin colour and background, and were too ashamed to confront such a situation. Exclusion was not poverty, but something that had damaged their identity, their sense of self-esteem.

The founding of Crear Vale la Pena

Inés realised, that in order to help these young people, decent institutions had to be developed within the poor districts themselves. There had to be places where youths could meet and educate themselves and, above all, foster their artistic expression. Furthermore, Inés hoped to be able to build up social networks in order to provide them with new securities. Such networks, she told us, are a matter of course in all other classes of society. They sustain people and help them to establish themselves.

After four years, in which Inés had worked together with the youths on single projects, she founded the organisation Crear Vale la Pena (or 'Creativity Pays Off') in 1997. The first cultural community centre in the poor district of Bajo Boulogne, Joven Creativo ('Creative Youth'), gave the people of the community a feeling that she was seriously concerning herself with them. And so, after initial scepticism, her work met with broad support. Before the year 2000, two more centres were opened, at which more than 1,000 students visited over 100 workshops annually.

The special atmosphere of Crear

Ten years later when we arrived at a dark, old building in a suburb of Buenos Aires we didn't know exactly who would meet us. While we waited, we looked through a slightly opened door into a large room. It must have been the dance studio: a solid wood floor, a large empty surface in the dim lighting, a guitar on the wall and a soft, diffuse beam of light gave us an idea of what life the room must hold during rehearsals. But that evening, all was quiet.

Suddenly, someone called us and accompanied us into a second-floor room full of work desks and performance posters. All at once, we found ourselves stood across from a group of people; they were talking on the phone, laughing, chattering and moving around, all full of activity. The tranquillity of the first floor was swept away. Someone waved us over and showed us a video about the organisation Crear Vale la Pena. The word 'crear' is powerful, as were the pictures of the performances that we were shown. We thought for a moment that this energy hardly had enough space in the one room, as a happy, curly-haired redhead of around 50 years of age rushed in through a hidden door.

'No revolution without joy, no joy without revolution,' Inés says often. And that is the impression she gave. She answered a few questions from her team members while gracefully moving by. Shortly thereafter, we sat in a cosy room with this energetic head of the organisation. We asked Inés why a successful dancer and choreographer would come up with an idea to give up her career and professionally dedicate herself to the poor of Buenos Aires. Why had she listened to her husband back then?

She replied sheepishly:

> I don't know exactly why I got involved. My devotion to passion, tension and movement carried me to the place where I'm standing today. Through Crear, I discovered a possibility for finding meaning in my daily life. As a child and as a professional dancer, I often felt very isolated – almost like the youths who I help today. I felt a sense of belonging for the first time in this organisation. And all of that gives me a great deal of energy and joy in life.

Personal maturity

Inés also explained to us that she had not actually given up her prior professional career, rather she had reinterpreted it in a different context. It was only from the year 2000 that she was personally ready to devote herself 100% to the work of Crear. Over the years, she had experienced more and more meaningfully how much more energy-packed and exciting the work in the poor districts was in contrast to her monotonous appearances on conventional stages:

> There is something that is not contemporary about contemporary dance, and it is the body. The body is not from today, it is from the time of Apollo, copied from Greek mythology. But if all professional dancers have the same bodies and have learned the same movements and routines, how can dance performances offer something new and innovative? I went from the ethic to the aesthetic. And the aesthetic was very much influenced by this idea of giving poor people access to dance. So we had to find a new way of choreographing, a new movement and a new dramaturgy because we were working with different bodies, different psychologies, different social backgrounds and different levels of education. I was more and more motivated by the work with the authentic artists in the slum.

When in 2000 the Avina Foundation[18] offered to financially support Inés if she concentrated fully on Crear, the decision was easy for her.

'Let's give rise to ideas, not names!'

Inés emphasised again and again that Crear is not just her, every success can only be a success if people work together. Inés quotes one of the last scenes from one of their plays:

> *Los heroes mueren bajo el peso de sus ideales*, which means: heroes die under the weight of their own ideas. There is a danger in building up leaders thinking that they can change the world. Of course, there will be actions carried out by people leading for a particular time. But there always needs to be collective action. Individual leaders in the last century inevitably got so much power that it was very difficult not to use this power for personal profit.

For that reason, Inés's slogan is: 'Let's give rise to ideas, not names!' In this vein, it was an important concern for her that the professional teachers she engaged for Crear would train the students to be instructors. And so, the number of trainers carrying on the spirit of Crear grew to over 60 and the team around Inés to 15. Inés told us that she wants not only to delegate and share the responsibility, but also the right to determine the future of the organisation.

Social transformation and democratic participation

The last seven years prior to our interview had been intense for Inés and she had often been brought almost to the edge of her capacities. 'Some people don't believe me, but there are moments when I feel unbelievably tired, maybe even depressed. But they usually go by quickly. My work is so full of life that you can't really become depressed.' Her joy in her daily work gives Inés so much energy, that she and her team have developed an entire series of projects for social transformation and democratic participation which revolve around education, art production, and the continuing development of the cultural community centres.

Democratic participation starts at Crear with the fact that the management team of the local cultural centres is composed of students and teachers from the centre itself. The neighbours from the districts should, for the most part, lead their centre independently and understand it as a network for solidarity.

---

18 Avina is a network of social entrepreneurs founded by Stephan Schmidheiny; please see www.avina.net/eng.

'Because of this,' Inés said, 'the communities are truly strengthened and benefit from self-confidence and a feeling of togetherness.' Crear also helps build outside relationships. Not only the connections with other poor districts are important, but also the connections with other social classes, members of government and not least with the businesses that financially support the work of Crear. All of these relationships represent a systematic approach to ending social exclusion and creating a new integration in Argentinian society. Of course, the many dance and music performances that the Crear students have given outside of their districts and abroad, for example in Germany, have helped in this. Through professional instruction in music, acting and visual art, many students have become so good that now their productions are also presented in the lofty theatres of Buenos Aires.

An international network for art and social transformation

Yet Inés wanted to achieve even more. Once transforming young lives with art got her hooked, she was no longer satisfied to nurture the exchange of experiences only within the centres she had established. She heard about other organisations in Latin America working on similar projects and, consequently, the idea of a network for art and social transformation was born. After four years of rather informal work, over 20 organisations met in 2007 in Santa Clara de la Sierra in order to share their experiences of social transformation through art and to learn from one another. According to Inés, this enabled all of them to take another step forward, bringing the movement onto the next level. In the future, she wants to withdraw herself somewhat from the operational business at Crear and work on making the ideas and experiences of the organisation transferable. Her aim is not to duplicate the model; rather she wants to share her experiences with other artists. What they do afterwards is up to them.

Passion, tension and movement

During our interview, Inés summarised once again, 'It is difficult to say what exactly has changed for me in the last few years. One thing is certain though: for me, art is connected to social transformation.' Even though she was satisfied with what she had been able to change through her abilities and through Crear in the poor districts of Buenos Aires and beyond, she was still aware that there was much more to be done:

> If revolution is not sexy, not connected to tenderness, if it doesn't smell good – it will never happen! Values are beautiful things! Propaganda builds sexy images driving people towards the business

world, to drugs, to violence and war. We could learn a lot from this, if we really want to change social reality.

Inés closed with an unexpected assertion: 'Let's remember the presence of death in life. Let's address it courageously. It makes life much easier – not harder. It's so simple to change things if you know that, no matter what, you have to die some day.'

Information

- www.crearvalelapena.org.ar
  Website of Crear Vale la Pena.

'In spite of my quick success and excellent prospects, I realised I wasn't doing what I was supposed to be doing. It was a quiet and uncertain feeling, but it was there and it grew stronger.'

Ashok Khosla
Physicist at Harvard
University, United Nations
functionary, sustainability
expert, professional job
creator
New Delhi, India

Ashok Khosla – The power of temptation

We heard about Ashok Khosla for the first time while in Berlin, in the magnificent, but sterile, Reichstag building. Ernst Ulrich von Weizsäcker, then a member of the German parliament, told us about a man who passed up high posts at Harvard and the United Nations (UN) to return to his Indian homeland with the intention of creating one million jobs. This sounded incredibly exciting, so we added New Delhi in our travel route in order to meet Ashok Khosla in person.

Four months later in 2005, we were travelling in what is typical for Delhi – a rickety, yellow, three-wheeled rickshaw through the outskirts of the city. In stark contrast to Berlin, it was hot and dusty with absolutely nothing magnificent about it. During the trip, a loud racket of cars and people surrounded us. Stray cows grazed here and there in a rubbish heap, others blocked the road. Our destination was the Qutab Institutional Area, where the current office of Development Alternatives is situated.

Unsure if we had arrived at our destination, we stood at a run-down building as a man dressed in traditional Indian attire passed by, fortunately, this was Ashok Khosla himself. After a quick greeting, he guided us towards the building to introduce his colleagues. After all, he was quick to explain, he himself wasn't so important, but the team was.

Everything here spoke of modesty – from the building and Ashok's simply equipped office, to his character. We made ourselves comfortable in a small room and after a short time we were under the spell of this warm-hearted, humble and highly intelligent man.

A prince from the suburbs

Born in northern Kashmir, Ashok's parents sent him, at the age of 14, to Cambridge for his schooling. After high school, he went on to study physics at Harvard, which he completed in record time. Soon after his graduation, the highly talented 23 year old was offered a position teaching physics and astronomy at Harvard. Additionally, he received an assignment to develop a new course of studies, 'People, Resources and Environment', from which the soon-to-be American vice president Al Gore was one of the first graduates.

Carried away by the speed with which he built a career, Ashok initially savoured the societal position that accompanied his job at Harvard, as well as the lucrative side jobs and intellectual challenges. As Ashok said, he was simply lucky to be in the right place at the right time – with the right skin colour. People from the former European colonies like India were, at the time, heavily supported.

'All these things offered me a life as a prince and so, at 31, after a few successful years at Harvard, I was in a place that most people could only dream of.' At that point in Ashok's story, we examined his room once again: aside from the full book shelves, not much there recalled his princely past. It must have been a long journey from the luxurious offices at Harvard all the way to this one that contained a rickety, scratched desk and bare concrete walls decorated only with a few newspaper clippings and pictures.

Environmental policy in India

Ashok continued: 'In spite of my quick success and excellent prospects, I realised I wasn't doing what I was supposed to be doing. It was a quiet and uncertain feeling, but it was there and it grew stronger.' Even if he didn't exactly know what he was really looking for, Ashok did not believe that he would find it at Harvard – even if he were to climb one or two rungs higher up the career ladder. Thus, in 1971 after eight interesting years in the USA, he decided to return to his homeland, India. After the time spent in the Western world, he suffered, as he calls it, a 'returner's burn-out'. Therefore the next thing Ashok did was withdraw to the beaches of Goa in south-west India, a fashionable location in the 1970s, to reflect on himself and on life. When, during this phase of reflection, he received an offer from the Indian government to develop the environmental department of the ministry for science and technology, he was unable to resist. And so, over the following four years, he devoted himself and all his strength to the development of the first Indian ministry for the environment. He enjoyed the task because he had always had a great interest in ecological subjects, as well as the desire to give something back to his home country. Soon the first successes came.

Yet, as the political and economic problems on the subcontinent became more intense, Indira Gandhi declared a state of emergency in 1975 and many civil liberties were limited. In this situation, Ashok could no longer pursue his work the way he envisioned it. So he determined to answer a request from the UN and develop the newly planned UN's environmental programme. So it was that Ashok left India in 1976 for the second time and headed for Nairobi.

Environmental policy on a global scale

The UN's project seemed to be exactly the right opportunity Ashok was looking for in order to collaborate on the improvement of international environmental standards. After his experiences at Harvard and in India, he was deeply certain that it was high time to take the ecologically explosive situation of the planet seriously. Ashok undertook responsibility for the development and establishment of Infoterra, the predecessor organisation of the United

Nations Environment Programme (UNEP). From Nairobi, the headquarters of the UNEP, he travelled tirelessly around the world to put ever more grave environmental problems on the agendas of international decision-makers and to attempt to move people to action. As he said himself, a person can become quite arrogant and presumptuous when he shakes the hands of international dignitaries every day.

However, with time, the feeling crept over Ashok that this fascinating task was luring him away from his true calling. While he flew around the globe on behalf of Infoterra, worldwide poverty increased daily and ecological problems became noticeably more menacing. This feeling of being seduced by money, power and a challenging job was all too familiar to him. But, in contrast to the time he had spent in Harvard, Ashok now knew what he wanted to do: he wanted to work on the core problem. The core problem was and is for Ashok, the fact that millions of poor people in developing countries – above all in his home country of India – have no possibility of earning a living for themselves. Not to mention the possibility of earning money in a way that is ecologically responsible.

Fighting poverty ecologically

In the year of 1983, Ashok took on the consequences of his thoughts and followed his inner voice: he wanted to approach the problem of poverty through the creation of jobs which also bore up under social and ecological criteria. In his opinion, fighting poverty required innovative approaches in development work. In the first place, it was necessary to supplant donations through a new combination of market stimulation, investment and technologies, which in the second place had to be specially tailored to the needs of poor people.

'It was in my DNA: it had to be possible to run development work as good as a successful business and it was my job to try it.' At the time, Ashok stood alone with this idea. In his opinion, the world system was and is structured in such a way that the poor grow poorer and the rich grow richer. Out of this develops an endless spiral of hopelessness, illness, hunger and finally violence – with a grave impact on the quality of life for many people.

Liberation from the poverty trap

In the same year, Ashok founded the organisation, Development Alternatives (DA). The goal of the organisation is to create opportunities for millions of people in the rural areas of India to earn a living wage, with consideration given to a socially and ecologically meaningful general framework. In the last 25 years, Ashok and his team have devoted themselves with persistence and tenacity to the task of finding and implementing solutions for this problem. The solutions conceptualised by DA are not developed for the one-time, short-term control of a problem. Rather, DA tries to establish models that have long-term positive social and ecological effects. Further, the solutions should be financially attractive and be able to be copied often. These solutions are tailored to small businesspeople: they have to make it possible for individuals, families or small groups to build up a business. Through the small income gained, a family can earn enough to liberate itself, with a first step out of the poverty trap.

A roofing tile for a better life

During a trip to Jhansi, a city about four-and-a-half hours from New Delhi, we got the opportunity to familiarise ourselves with some of DA's initiatives. We made our way in an almost unbearable 47°C to a rural branch of DA on dusty streets glowing with the heat. We saw people everywhere with their heads wrapped in fabric cloths to protect their ears from dirt and heat. Someone explained to us that, during these high temperatures, the ears are most quickly affected.

We reached the village centre, which – in contrast to the surroundings – seemed relatively green and friendly. From our air-conditioned car we went directly into an air-conditioned room, grateful that we only had to spend a short time in the glaring sun. We were not spared for long, however, since we had to go out to meet some workers, who, only protected by a small shelter, were being trained in the manufacture of roofing tiles.

In groups of five to ten people, they learned which raw materials were necessary for the production of the tiles. They learned how to store them and how to use simple tools. On an additional course, the future small businesspeople were taught how they could build up a small, profitable factory around the production process. Even if the area made an inhospitable and hostile impression on us and the buildings in the town seemed makeshift – building materials are always needed. The self-made tiles found buyers among the poorest people in Jhansi, just as in many other areas of India.

In Jhansi, not only roofing tile manufacture was being taught. Using weeds gathered by the poorest of the poor, two generators were operated to provide environmentally friendly power for the guest house, the paper factory and other small factories. The paper was made from crushed cotton leftovers, and indigenous fruits were made into stews and juices. In one other factory, young people learned how to build small ovens newly designed by DA, which ensured that highly poisonous cooking smoke no longer lingered in the huts, but could be channelled outdoors. All these technologies had been developed especially for local needs. This also meant that they had to be extremely low-priced in order to allow them to be developed into successful business models. Only in this way would they be bought by the poor, yet discerning population.

Women's networks and satellite dishes

After viewing a micro-credit project, some small dams, and a tile factory, we visited one of the many women's groups organised by DA. Through their community-building character, the women's group we met helped rural women to gain self-reliance. Sooner or later they found themselves getting together in small groups to develop businesses with the help of a small loan.

Finally, we became witnesses of the victorious march of information technology into rural India. In two small villages beyond driveable roads, we visited two of the 50 TARAhaats built up by DA: these were small computer schools, in which the population could learn English along with computer use. The building had no windows and no telephone, only a satellite antenna on the roof. With the help of specially developed computer programs, some of the people were learning reading and writing. The TARAhaat also offered completely new services to the residents. These included micro-insurance for poor harvests and also market information on the current price of manufactured wares.

Fighting poverty as a life calling

In the projects all around Jhansi, the energy with which Ashok and his team spurred DA's mission onwards was palpable. It is uplifting to experience their strategies in reality. It is bolstering to see the innovations through which tailored technologies and the sensible use of resources offer new chances for so many people.

If you look more closely at the DA world, a multifaceted spectrum of business initiatives is unfolded. The examples described briefly above are but a small part of what Ashok has initiated in the last few years. For example, DA has pointed out ways in which houses and other products can be created out of native bamboo. The organisation has developed mini-electric plants run on renewable biomass fuel. New projects are being built with partners, such as ZERI, which are intended to solve entire problem cycles in the areas of energy, water and mobility.[19]

19 ZERI stands for 'Zero Emissions Research and Initiatives' and is a network of over 3,000 scientists, system analysts and experts around the world. These people develop solutions through which rubbish from one part of a system can be used as fuel for another part (see www.zeri.org).

If you could experience the enthusiasm and energy with which Ashok Khosla and his team reported on the various initiatives, you would sense that here is a person who has found his life's calling. Ashok affirmed this with satisfaction: 'I did not really make a choice – it was written, it was genetic. For a while I was successfully running away, though – during my education and then career I got seduced by success, by knowledge, richness, power, ego trips and taking the easy way.'

Personal career priorities

If you consider the fact that Ashok could have had, with high certainty, a career at one of the most renowned American universities or at the UN, his decision might seem like a sacrifice. But according to Ashok, nothing in the world could have made him happier or more satisfied than being able to see every day that his work finds a practical and long-term path out of poverty for more and more people.

Of course there are only a few jobs in the world that could be more difficult, draining and sometimes frustrating. The implementation of the projects was difficult in the rural areas, it was sometimes unsuccessful and took longer than desirable. The capital required was large and Ashok often had a hard time finding the money required for pilot projects or large invested expansions. Yet, in spite of all the set-backs and difficulties, he is happy that he had the courage to found DA. In the meantime, DA's work has benefited more than two million people, especially women, in various ways. Many have been able to improve the conditions of their lives, others to build up a sustainable living.

At the close of our conversation, Ashok said:

> I know that I will fail to meet my big goal – eradicating poverty – during my life time. So, my job is to set up the machine as long as I am here. With it, one can only hope that the world will succeed.

Information

- www.devalt.org, www.tarahaat.com, www.dainet.org
  Websites of Development Alternatives.

- www.khosla.in
  Ashok Khosla's personal website.

- www.unep.org
- www.wwf.org
- www.cluboframe.de
- www.wbcsd.org
  Information about organisations in the area of sustainability.

'I know that I'm helping build a better world for my own children. That inspires me more than all of the money and power in the world.'

Erin Keown Ganju
Asia aficionado, investment banker, entrepreneur, promoter of education
San Francisco, USA

Erin Keown Ganju – No signposts pointing to happiness

Erin Keown Ganju, Californian born, inherited from her father a passion for foreign cultures, languages and, not least, for business. He was a professor of international marketing who instructed all around the world. Erin's mother was one of the first volunteers in the American Peace Corps in the 1960s. From her, Erin gained sensitivity and a desire to care for the weaker members of society.

Erin has always been true to the family tradition of wanting to explore the world. She was fascinated by Asia as early as high school, and she studied Chinese and travelled extensively.

Goldman Sachs and the international metropolis of finance

Erin finished her college degree in international relations with honours at an elite university in Washington. Next, she followed in the footsteps of her father. Her experiences on her many travels, as well as her studies, convinced her of the great influence of private businesses on the lives and cultures of many people worldwide. It would be worth it to acquaint herself intimately with this world. And what would be more ideal for this than investment banking on Wall Street, the epitome of the capitalist system and the place on which the economic information of the entire world converged? Up to this point in her life, Erin had only begrudgingly settled for mediocrity. So she went to Goldman Sachs, one of the leading investment banks worldwide. She threw herself into work there, often without really being aware of where her office was. Her desk was in New York one day, then in Hong Kong the next and later on in Singapore. She had insane work hours; 80 plus hours per week, including weekends. There was no time for friends or for getting to know countries and cultures. But when a person is young, enjoys work and likes to measure her success by how big the last transaction or bonus was, she played the game with passion.

And yet, at 26 and still quite young, after some years in high finance Erin realised that Goldman Sachs was a fantastic training camp, but not her life's passion. The work, often abstract and seemingly distant from reality, under-taken in anonymous palaces of glass, could not be the only thing in life. She also realised that every day it would become harder to resist the pull of ever increasing wages. So, she resigned from her post in Singapore without really knowing exactly what she would do next. She only knew that she would like to live in a developing country and spend a great deal of time learning to understand the land and its people.

Unilever and development projects in Vietnam

Sometimes life gives you what you're looking for. At exactly the right time, Erin heard that Unilever, one of the largest food product concerns in the world, wanted to build up its business anew in Vietnam. She seized the opportunity, and three exciting years in Ho Chi Minh City, formerly known as Saigon, followed. Now she had time to concern herself with local problems such as education and health care and get to know the local people, especially since Unilever considered it important to gain the trust of the population and to build up a positive image during its launch phase. Erin supported the construction of nurseries, health centres and schools with happiness and enthusiasm. Doing this, she discovered talents in herself that she had never used before. In spite of the multifaceted projects, Erin returned to her Californian home town in 1997, open to the opportunities that would open up for her.

Internet start-ups and frenzy in Silicon Valley

When Erin arrived in San Francisco, she was pulled into the riptide of the Internet boom. Looking back, she says it was a crazy time. You could walk down the streets of Silicon Valley and hop from one top position into the next. Nothing was the same as it had been before, gone was the time when you had to prove yourself to a large corporation through decades of work before you could rise to positions of responsibility with their own budget. Erin immediately received a job as an executive responsible for international business development. She began to fly around the world again, hurrying from one appointment to the next. She bought up businesses in ten countries within one year and helped her own company launch its first public offering on the market in the same year. The company's progress was too much, too fast and it ended in a fiasco. Erin's company wasn't worth anything; her share became so-called penny stocks. After this quick roller-coaster ride from boom to bust, she was immediately hired by the next start-up, again as an executive responsible for international development. Once more, however, the share price of the enterprise shot up and then plummeted down.

As Erin explained to us, at the time, she was, at barely 30 years of age, too young to resist the classical model of success. Success was measured by whether you could keep up financially in a highly turbulent, highly paid work environment. It made a good impression to talk about the last big international company purchase and the new Ferrari at a cocktail party. This unbelievable pace generated permanent stress and barely left time for conscious personal decisions to be made.

The decisive questions

Within three years, Erin experienced the complete life cycle of the start-up twice: from swift expansion, to market frenzy, to the crash and all the while endless hours of work. She felt completely burned out and, for the first time, she asked herself consciously what she actually wanted to do with her life. Did she want to keep running in this rat race, faster and faster, in the hopes of outlasting the competition? Did she want to change over to the next new enterprise and apply what she had learned, probably just until the next crash? Did she really want to put her energy into that? What did 'success' mean for her personally? What had given her the most joy in the last ten years, where had she found the greatest personal fulfilment?

To her surprise, Erin realised that the answers to these questions didn't have anything to do with Goldman Sachs, her high income, good jobs, or luxury. Her most positive memories were those she had of her work in Vietnam. There she had helped people in the country change their lives, and she had felt real joy doing it.

The search for the right change

Erin decided to obey herself. She decided to start a new chapter in her life. But what was it exactly that she wanted to do? She began to search, to have thoughts and discuss them with her friends. One of them put her in contact with John Wood. John, like Erin, had had a high-flying career at Microsoft in the last seven years. But, over time, he too came to the insight that he no longer wanted to use his abilities for big money and career-making. Rather, he wanted to support people who had fewer chances than himself.

Very quickly, the two saw that they had acquired similar attitudes towards many questions due to their comparable experiences. John told her that he had founded a non-profit enterprise, 'Books for Nepal', in order to improve the chances of Nepalese children through education. When he mentioned that he would like to introduce the programme into additional countries, Erin felt that this was the task she was looking for. Because John and Erin also realised that they had a very similar understanding of how a successful organisation should be run, the cornerstone was laid for a shared future. She wanted to contribute to lowering the shocking statistic of 120 million children worldwide who were not able to attend an elementary school. Both John and Erin were convinced: positive change in the world begins with education for children.

Sharing the work and professional expansion

Since the name 'Books for Nepal' wasn't quite right for developing the organisation in multiple countries, Erin and John transformed the initiative into the non-profit enterprise 'Room to Read' in 2001. John's job was to find more donors. He has been rather successful in this: the budget increased from US$200,000 in 2001 to around US$6 million in 2006.

Erin occupied herself with the development of the following five programmes and their expansion in other countries. Her job included the foundation of schools and bilingual libraries in close cooperation with the local communities, the publication of children's books in local languages, the development of computer and language labs, and the accommodation of girls with long-term scholarships. Her side of the enterprise has an almost unbelievable success story. All parts of the programme have been established in six countries in Asia, and since 2006, in two African countries. Room to Read has improved the lives of 1.2 million children in Cambodia, Laos, India, Nepal, Sri Lanka, Vietnam, Zambia and South Africa. All of these countries have one thing in common: the majority of the population has to get by on US$1 per day.

The local teams that Erin coordinates from San Francisco have opened over 3,600 libraries, built 287 schools, printed 1.4 million children's books in local languages, and have built and furnished 117 computer and language labs. Room to Read has donated an additional 1.4 million English-language books and has financed 2,336 multiple-year scholarships for girls – these numbers grow every day.

Factors for success and local personalities

According to Erin, all of this was only possible because she and John worked in a results-oriented way from the very beginning, just as they had in their earlier business lives. The experiences they had gained in the business world were invaluable for their large-scale projects.

Each project in the Room to Read system is led by a local team and must be supported by the community that benefits from it. And it is important that nothing comes completely free. The citizens of the community only take on the responsibility and value the projects when they themselves have contributed significantly – through their labour, through the preparation of land and building materials, or through money. If these local contributions do not cover at least 30% of the total cost, Room to Read will not even begin the project. This also serves the purpose of making it clear to people from the beginning that they will not be supported forever. At some point they must be in a position to continue their projects independently. And previous experiences show that they do reach that point.

Priceless beauty

We wanted to know whether Erin had ever missed the business world. 'Sometimes', she admitted, 'but seldom,' for example, when she wants to buy a house in San Francisco, which is no simple matter with the real estate prices common there. She told us however, that her doubts dissolve whenever she thinks about the satisfaction that she experiences in her work. Whenever she visits the hard-working people abroad and sees what they are in the process of growing, she perceives these as moments of priceless beauty.

Education work is, for Erin, the most important opportunity for giving disadvantaged people the chance to lead a self-determined life. For that reason, it is currently unthinkable to her to return to the typical business world. Today she measures her success by other numbers: numbers with real people behind them. Numbers like the number of children who are able to read or to attend schools. Erin is eager to come to work every day – a feeling that she barely knew in her first ten years of work.

Erin knows that she is helping to build a better world for her own children too. This gives her more inspiration than all the money and power in the world, and as she told us, she was already looking forward to the day when she could show her one year old daughter what Room to Read has created for many other children.

Information

- www.roomtoread.org
  Room to Read's website including the latest news.

- www.huffingtonpost.com/erin-ganju
  Erin Ganju's profile and blog posts.

'Balancing legitimate financial needs with a socially responsible job – this is one of the most important themes in my life. I try to learn from people who have achieved the seemingly impossible.'

Jordan Kassalow
Optometrist, development
aid doctor, policy strategist,
entrepreneur
New York, USA

Jordan Kassalow – Using your own potential

Jordan Kassalow, a New York optometrist, describes his original perspective on life:

> I could actually work my entire life as a successful eye doctor and optometrist in New York. My father had a successful practice, right in Manhattan. But what effects would my life have, how much of my potential will I have really lived out?

However, an internship in Mexico showed Jordan further possibilities hidden in his profession.

Just having fun, not playing God

Jordan recalls his years as a student:

> My original intent on applying for an internship with a developmental aid organisation was to go have a cool experience, travel the world, and learn some of my new clinical skills. It wasn't really driven by wanting to save the world.

Back then, Jordan had no idea that he would experience things even on his very first day of work that would change his life forever. On this first day, a six-year-old blind boy was sent to him for treatment.

> I was looking at him and everything wasn't really adding up, so I pulled one of my professors over. After a while a professor and I discovered that the boy was not blind, but profoundly near-sighted, a -22. I went to our catalogue of 5,000 glasses and found a very strong pair of glasses for him. When I put them on, his face went from this blank stare to becoming animated and for the first time in his life, this boy saw the world with all of its contours and colours. His life had changed – and so had mine.

A further moving experience was an encounter with a deeply religious elderly woman. She came to the office complaining that she had been unable to read the Bible for ten years – prior to this, it had been her comfort and support in life. The woman had only a slight weakness of vision, typical for her age, and with a simple pair of reading glasses that Jordan gave her; he gave her the opportunity to read again.

> I went into work the next morning, it was like seven in the morning and there was a big long line and there she was, the woman waiting in line with 20 chickens. She had brought me 20 chickens as a present. For me I was just giving her a pair of reading glasses, but for her it was like I had given her God back.

These experiences pointed out the way for Jordan to discover his life's goal and purpose: he did not want to become an eye doctor in order to earn big money, but rather so that he could use his abilities to improve the lives of other people and, above all, the lives of the underprivileged.

Apprenticeship years in Asia, South America and Africa

But how was Jordan supposed to approach his newly discovered life mission? For the moment it seemed a good idea to finish his studies and gain career experience. Before he finished his doctorate in ophthalmology at the New England College in New York, he wrote a letter to Dr V, the man who had revolutionised cataract treatment and who had pioneered an affordable treatment for this age-related eye problem for the populations of developing countries. Dr V and his enterprise Aravind Eye Care (see p. 52) fascinated Jordan so deeply that he offered to work for the older doctor for free, if his cost of living could be covered. After a year with Dr V, Jordan had learned very much first-hand what ophthalmology for the poorest of the poor means.

He returned to the USA in order to complete a graduate degree in public health at the John Hopkins University, after which he returned to developing countries. First, Jordan went to Bolivia for a year in order to examine blindness in children for a medical study. On the basis of this knowledge, the Helen Keller International Foundation offered him a position as director for Onchocerciasis (or river blindness) in Africa. The offer was a good opportunity for Jordan to unite his financial needs with the desire to pursue an altruistic goal in his job. During the next eight years, he led a team of up to 50 people in 19 African countries with the purpose of curbing river blindness.

Health policy as foreign policy

In Africa, Jordan learned a great deal about possibilities to improve local health structures even with very small financial means. Yet money was always lacking when it came to solving problems in the long term. Jordan had to recognise that the political lobby for health matters was weak. His conclusion was that health must receive higher international regard. Only in this way would there be a chance to accumulate a budget for eliminating the most urgent problems.

Over the years, it became clear to Jordan that health policy is not only about the treatment of illnesses. More than that, it is an economic matter, a matter of foreign policy and security policy – and it has to be understood that way internationally too. For example, a quarter of all people today worldwide, 1.6 billion, have no access to corrective lenses. This causes a huge loss of productivity. For this reason alone, a majority of the people thus affected are closed out of gainful employment and condemned to a life of hardship. Similar, if not worse, are the economic consequences of HIV/AIDS, malaria, tuberculosis and other diseases which are treatable and curable yet lead to a fatal end in thousands of cases every day. In South Africa, for example, many jobs are double-hired because even in hiring one has to figure in the AIDS death rate from the very beginning.

Money or passion – an either–or situation?

As a consequence of these considerations, Jordan decided after some years to give up his career as a doctor in development aid in order to work on repositioning the topic of health at the political level. Committed to his idea, Jordan organised a meeting with the director of an independent think-tank, the Council for International Relations in Washington, to explain his ideas. This challenged Jordan to make a convincing case for his conclusions with only one small presentation. The study had to have made a big an impression as Jordan was given the task of developing a health policy department for this famous American think-tank. Over the next five years, he had conversations and discussions with countless business people, politicians and all the influential people who would listen to him. He liked the work, even though he missed the close connection to people that he had felt and treasured during his years of work in Africa, South America and Asia.

In all of these discussions and conferences, it continually occurred to Jordan that the workers of banks and NGOs envied each other. The bankers and lawyers wished for nothing more than a deeper meaning in their jobs, while the NGO workers wanted to be able to afford the material lifestyle of the banker and lawyers. This recurring observation almost forced Jordan towards the question of whether it was really an either–or situation: either you earn a lot, or you follow your passion. He told us: 'Balancing legitimate financial needs with a socially responsible job – this is one of the most important themes in my life. I try to learn from people who have achieved the seemingly impossible'.

Affordable luxury – designs for everyone

After five years of successful work at the Council for International Relations, Jordan began to develop his own answer to this challenging question. With the help of a colleague, he founded the enterprise Scojo Vision and the charitably-oriented Scojo Foundation. Scojo Vision seeks to offer affordable glasses with high-quality design in industrialised countries. Jordan had discovered a market gap here: 'Either the glasses are beautiful and expensive, or you get a cheap, heavy frame.' When we met him, he had, for the last five years, been selling attractive and innovatively designed glasses at prices between €7 and €70. He showed us some in the New York Scojo office. The products are sold in multiple eyeglass store chains in the USA, among other places. But what, we wondered, had become of Jordan's passion for helping people in developing countries?

Glasses for a dollar

Jordan told us that there was a similar need in India and Africa. There too, people want good glasses at an affordable price. For this need, there is the Scojo Foundation, which finances itself through donations and through a portion of the profits from Scojo Vision. The foundation offers glasses for age-related near-sightedness in developing countries at prices between US$1 and $3. In order to make these prices possible, the foundation trains so-called 'Scojo entrepreneurs', who are outfitted with a 'store in a suitcase'. After a basic training, they can carry out vision testing and sell the right glasses directly to customers in the isolated villages in which they live. Frequently they sell only very simple reading glasses, such as you would find at kiosks or in the supermarket in the industrialised world, but such glasses make an immense difference to people's lives.

The Scojo Foundation works as a franchising partner with social entrepreneurs in many countries. The local partners are trained and they, in turn, train Scojo entrepreneurs in their region. In the beginning, they tried to work with micro-loans from third parties in order to make the start-up investment of about €60 affordable. The administrative effort required, however, was too great and the micro-loans were replaced by a system in which Scojo requires a single small deposit and, after that, the initial equipment is given to the new Scojo entrepreneur without any special conditions. The entrepreneur then pays back the start-up investment slowly out of funds coming from the sale of the first pairs of glasses. Thus far, no one has taken advantage of the foundation's trust, Jordan told us; so it appears that the system functions quite successfully.

The fact that the Scojo Foundation doesn't simply directly sell the glasses, but instead shapes their distribution through many small Scojo entrepreneurs who are trained and supported, contributes a great deal to its success and swift growth. In this way, the Scojo glasses have an exponentially positive effect: to begin with, the customers profit through affordable access to a high-quality product. In addition, awareness about eye diseases is increased and jobs are created and maintained, not only for the micro-entrepreneurs, but also for the customers, who with the help of glasses, can begin or continue working.

The role of women and the financing of vision

In the development of the programme in new countries, Scojo works consciously to find the right entrepreneurs. The main target group in this effort is women. By giving women, who are often strongly disadvantaged, the possibility to earn or supplement their income through a small business selling glasses, they and their children automatically receive access to health services, education and adequate food. This leads in the long term to an educated, healthy and more peaceful society.

Currently, the Scojo Foundation is represented in Guatemala, India, El Salvador, Bangladesh and India. In the coming years it is important for Jordan to make access to Scojo glasses a possibility for a majority of people in further developing countries. The long-term financing plan of the foundation allows for financing the operations of individual country programmes from the profits of the Scojo entrepreneurs. The expenses of the headquarters in New York will be covered out of the profit of the Scojo Vision business, which is currently about 5% of the profit each year. New programmes and the development of a Scojo infrastructure in further countries will be financed by donations.

Jordan is satisfied with his work and plans to continue to invest his energy in a combination of business and innovative support for developing countries,

> Looking up after a long day with a line of patients as far as my eye can see, I realised: I could sit here for the rest of my life. So I started asking myself, am I most efficient sitting here or would it be more beneficial if someone else was sitting here and I could do something else? I have other strengths, I'm a good fundraiser, I'm good at building bridges, telling stories about the other side of the world. I like fieldwork, but I don't feel like that's where I can ultimately give my best value.

Since he gets to do a little bit of everything these days, Jordan is content. With Scojo Vision, the foundation and occasional work in his father's practice, he has been successful in realising his life goal: he can cover his financial needs and use his abilities so that they benefit disadvantaged people. Jordan is certain that he will be able to look back on his life and feel good. Thoughtfully he suggests: 'When you're lying in your deathbed, that's not the time to say I shoulda, coulda, woulda. But today, if there are any shoulda, coulda, wouldas in your life you better get to them, because time passes fast.'

Personal freedom and the potential of the individual

Jordan's engagement has only one disadvantage – he works a lot. This is no sacrifice, but rather a conscious choice, and as long as the work can be balanced with his other priorities, above all with his family, he is happy. He solves the problem thus: after an evening break with his family he works late into the night. When we asked him about his motivation, he answered without pausing to think:

> All over the world I have recognised one basic motivation for people: they want a better life for their children. When I see people who are starting out with so much less then I had, I'm compelled to do what I can to help, because I've been afforded with so many gifts. Another thing I value is the personal freedom to follow my passion and live out my potential, it's very important to me. I see people all around the world who have no chance of getting close to their potential. That's what motivates me.

Further, he said:

> Probably the most intellectual foundation of my motivation is that I simply enjoy creating things and solving problems. I see a simple product that is needed by millions and billions of people around the world and they just don't have it.

Information

- www.visionspring.org
  Scojo was rebranded as Vision Spring.

- Prahalad, C.K., and H.C. Fruehauf (2006) *Der Reichtum der Dritten Welt* (*The Wealth of the Third World*) (Munich: Financial Publishing).

CONCLUSION

Six insights and experiences are presented here from Chapter 4.

1. Meaningless success and power can lead to short-term satisfaction, at times they can even leave you in trance. However, in the long run, they will not lead to happiness. A full bank account is neither our primary reason for existence nor our ultimate purpose in life

2. In order to reach true success you have to invest some serious thought into the question of what your goals in life and your personal values are

3. When you are already successful in a certain field it sometimes seems hard to imagine that you could also be successful in another field. This is when prior success turns into an obstacle for your own happiness. It can, however, turn out that your previous career was a prerequisite for the new, meaningful one. Use your skills!

4. Your essential goals often assume a clear shape if you think from the other end: What do you want to look back on? What is truly important, considering that our existence is essentially fleeting?

5. It is never too late to change course: Aims can be corrected, and with some courage you can give your life a new direction

6. Some successful people start a second career after shifting their lives in a new direction. They often capitalise on the same abilities, talents and networks that made them successful the first time

5

'What will others think of me?'

We are all coined by the places where we grow up or the environment we live in. Education, schooling, the circle of friends and our families have a strong influence on our thoughts, actions and feelings. And our personal value set is decisively determined by our social context – whether we like it or not.

It requires a lot of resolve and self-confidence to represent convictions and opinions that differ from the norm and it is even harder to live by them. Sometimes one can turn into an outsider or meet with a shake of head, an eye of suspicion and a lack of understanding.

These difficulties are well known to the people portrayed in the following chapter. But only by moving outside of the pre-existing paradigms, norms and values were they able to succeed on their own way. They trusted their inner voice, their passions and convictions. Over time their perseverance even led sceptical friends, colleagues and relatives to change their minds. Some of them developed a healthy respect for their work – and even supported their initiatives at a later point in time.

These are the stories of people who shaped their journey by staying true to themselves, even in the face of strong opposition.

'Even if it kills me tomorrow, there's nothing better that I can do with my life.'

Roma Debabrata
Dancer, professor, activist
against human trafficking,
mother of 40
New Delhi, India

Roma Debabrata – The healing effects of a poisonous injection

Roma Debabrata's father, a respected Indian government officer, and her mother, who grew up as the child of well-to-do landowners, were very proud of their daughter. She was on the right path to becoming a celebrated prima ballerina. Since her sixth year of life, Roma had received instruction in classical dance. She breezed through her schoolwork and her thoughts about world improvement, which flared up now and again, made her mother, who had always engaged herself for the needy of Calcutta, happy.

However at 21 years of age, Roma decided almost overnight to give up dance. 'How was it possible to worry about pointe shoes, while surrounded by wretched dwellings and omnipresent hunger?', she thought to herself. She could not recognise what meaning an existence as a dancer could have for the daily misery in the streets of Calcutta. 'How can it be that millions have to suffer, while I indulge a tiny elite as a prima ballerina? It didn't make any sense for me anymore,' Roma recalled when we spoke to her in the first half of 2005. Her decision, however, was met with incomprehension by her traditionally minded parents.

Years of being misunderstood

Alongside dancing, Roma had completed a master's degree in literature. She decided to become a literature instructor at the University of New Delhi. Everyone around her was shocked with her decision: Roma not only rode roughshod over the possibility of an extraordinary career, she also moved away from her family, which was completely unusual for the 1960s in India. This however, changed nothing about Roma's decision. In the years that followed, she enjoyed teaching literature in a way that helped students recognise the contradictions that existed in their society. Roma tried to expand her students' world-view beyond literature and to make them aware of the social realities in their own country. Simultaneously, Roma was part of a university group that organised volunteer social projects. 'Somehow I always knew that I wanted to change things. Circumstances that inflict emotional and psychological pain on people especially bothered me because that is dehumanising,' Roma told us. Many people expressed their concern about the fate of mistreated fellow citizens. But often this was founded in a patronising, pitying attitude which failed to recognise truly the right of these people to humane treatment. And only a few people followed up on their concerns with concrete action.

Backing makes you courageous

The resistance from her parents and her acquaintances did not prevent Roma from doing what she believed to be right. In this, her good earnings as a professor and the support of her husband helped. Her husband, an engineer, came from a family that was engaged in union organisation and actively supported the women's movement. Here Roma found understanding and backing for her work. 'They stood behind me like a rock,' she recalled.

In the years that followed, Roma become ever more involved on behalf of the socially disadvantaged. When she looked into the streets of New Delhi, she felt so privileged to have enjoyed a good education and to be able to work daily at the university that she felt a deep need to give something back.

Roma believes that her engagement was influenced by her mother. In contrast to her, however, she wanted to change her life and come into much more direct contact with people. During most of the years of her life, Roma worked as a professor and enjoyed family time. One of her dreams was to have 11 daughters, but she only had one biological daughter. During this time she had the desire to become more intensively involved in social work. But for many years she didn't know exactly in what form and in which area she should concentrate her efforts.

The positive effect of poison

In 1992, Roma was asked by a lawyer friend whether she had time to accompany him to a court session in order to translate the testimony of an abused 14-year-old girl. She agreed to it spontaneously. As Roma later learned, the lawyer feared that the testimony of the girl would be falsely rendered by the official interpreter. The young Bengali woman was sold to a man at ten years of age. The man had promised her parents to make a better life possible for her in the city. This 'better life' meant being raped daily, not only by the man she had been sold to, but also by a number of other men, over multiple years. Among her tormentors were police officers, which ensured that the illegal prostitution of this minor was kept secret – a tragic fact, which is unfortunately no exception.

Thanks to Roma's interpretation, the girl's testimony before the court could not be falsified. The girl identified the people who had abused her. There was a tumult in the courtroom. Roma intuitively felt a threat and protected the young woman by placing herself in front of her. At the same moment, she felt a stabbing pain in her back and fell to the floor. In the turmoil, a poisonous injection had been rammed into her spine, apparently intended for the girl. Roma was partially paralysed and spent three months in great pain in hospital before she overcame the consequences of the attack.

'And then I knew what I woke up for every day'

We met Roma when she was 58 years old, in her simple office on the out-skirts of New Delhi. A young woman listened with interest and now and again someone popped in to get a signature or a good word. Roma spoke with a soft, but very certain voice:

> My whole life I had looked for a job that would give my life purpose. And in that moment, when I was almost poisoned because I had protected an abused child, I knew what I would do for the rest of my life. I don't believe that I will change the world. I only want to contribute to making the life of some disadvantaged women and children a little bit better.

Since that moment in the courtroom, Roma has felt a tenacity and strength in herself that she would never have believed possible.

STOP: For stopping what shouldn't be

In order to fulfil her newly discovered life mission, Roma founded the organi-sation STOP (Stop Trafficking and Oppression of Children and Women) in 1997. When we interviewed her, the teams, which had then grown to 20 peo-ple, and the many volunteers had set themselves the goal of putting an end to the trafficking of children and women and the human tragedy linked to it. Their work is not only to liberate the girls from the basements of the bordello owners. STOP helps the survivors to rebuild their own lives – through educa-tion and vocational programmes, new homes and new work opportunities. Roma expressed it this way:

> These children are kidnapped, sold, forced to have sex and abused for money. Now, when they are rescued, they have the right to make their own choices about what they want to do, who they want to be, for the first time. We support them in this as best we can.

One of the most important things STOP does is procure information about the hideaways of trafficked minority-aged children. Then a quick and dan-gerous raid together with the police takes place in order to get as many girls as possible out of the hands of the child abusers. Roma became almost rest-less as she described it:

> It is mainly our role to acquire information about where girls are hidden. In this we are helped by our expansive network of part-ner organisations, doctors, volunteers, sometimes clients and even rickshaw-drivers in the city's neighbourhoods. In order to liberate the girls, we then organise raids that have to be carried out with almost military precision. If we are not quick, the traces of the girls

are often lost forever. When you lose a child here, you've lost her forever.

For such rescue actions, girls who have themselves survived similar situations are best suited. They are quick and nimble, are well-acquainted with such places and find the hideaways in the shortest time. Some of the girls rescued by Roma in past years are carefully trained so that they can confront their trauma yet again in order to help other children.

In a mixture of shock, awe and admiration, our gazes swept towards the young woman who had listened to our conversation calmly and with deep concentration. Roma continued,

> After liberating them, we accompany the girls to the police and to medical examinations, because they are afraid they will be brought back again – unfortunately, this thought is not without justification. We make sure that the girls are treated well by the police, that their meagre possessions do not disappear, that no bribes are taken and that the girls are taken to safe locations before their cases go to trial. After that we support them through our rehabilitation programmes.

To the question of whether her plans are dangerous and whether she is sometimes afraid, she answered simply: 'Even if it kills me tomorrow, there's nothing better that I can do with my life.' She worries sometimes about the safety of her one biological daughter, who now works for the UN and is convinced that Roma should make no compromises when it comes to her work.

Millions of girls sold

The shocking annual number reported by the UN of four million girls worldwide who have a fate similar to the girl whom Roma translated for in court shows that Roma's work is more than essential. According to an estimate of the Indian government, two million children between the ages of five to 15 were forced into sexual exploitation in 2005. They are sold by their families under false pretences for a piece of bread or given as would-be brides to sex traffickers in disguise. In India the shameful number of 500,000 children is added onto this figure yearly. Annually, US$5 billion are generated through the sexual exploitation of children. Thousands of children are trafficked from Nepal to India every year.

The dream of daughters fulfilled

At the time of our interview, Roma is happy. She puts her university income into STOP. She herself does not need much to live on. Her sari, traditional Indian clothing, costs US$3. She doesn't need more than four hours of sleep and this she allows herself often only in her desk chair. Her extended family takes care of food. Even this dream she has fulfilled for herself. Our conversation was interrupted by a young couple who seemed to have something urgent to discuss. After a while, the three embrace each other and a short discussion followed, after which the young people left the room with broad smiles. Roma explained that the young man asked her for permission to marry her 'daughter'. She told us that she had consented, but must however still make sure that the young woman is treated well and is allowed to have her own freedom to make decisions. Like many of the other 45 women who live with Roma and whom she now calls 'daughters', this young woman earned a driver's licence and would like to work as a taxi driver. Her future husband is sceptical, but no one can take this success away from her.

Roma's daughters live in the house of her extended family, built with donations. There, they learn English, cooking, gardening, driving and much more. The goal is for them to develop into self-confident and independent people, not to remain victims. Roma spends a great deal of time there, in order to truly realise the mother role. Of the girls, 17 are already married. Roma went on to tell us that she is convinced that,

> This is the life that I always wanted for myself. I always wanted to have many children, now I am surrounded by lovable girls who I can help and whose growth I watch over. I am now almost 60 years old. I work daily for the right things and there is still much to be done. Every day is a new day, not a leftover from yesterday.

Information

- www.stopindia.org
  Website of STOP.

- www.maitinepal.org
  Website of the Nepalese partner organisation.

- www.crin.org
  Children's Rights Information Network.

'At the end of my life, I want simply to be able to look into the eyes of my grandchildren and tell them reassuringly that grandpa did everything he could. This motivation is enough.'

David Suzuki
Nature lover, geneticist, TV
darling, visionary
Vancouver, Canada

David Suzuki – Visions for grandchildren

David Suzuki sat before us, casually dressed in jeans and a lumber-jack shirt, laid back as he leant in an easy-chair. He responded to our questions with answers that were ready for press. Other interviewees had already told us about this astonishing man, who has informed and fascinated Canadians for more than three decades with the work of his foundation, countless television and radio series and books about environmental topics. Yet how could it come to this, that the child of Japanese parents, born in 1936 in Vancouver, could go from star geneticist to the embodiment of a more sustainable future for Canada?

A doctorate in zoology

David told us that extensive camping and fishing trips with his father as a child influenced him strongly. He loved to spend hours with nature. He could not see enough of new plants and animals. Because of his love for nature, it was no difficult decision for him to complete a doctorate in zoology after finishing his college education in Amherst with honours in 1958. He owed his opportunity to complete his doctoral education in Chicago, USA, more to happy coincidence than to deliberate planning. This was, as would become clear, a lucky case, since at the time the academic level in the USA was significantly higher than in Canada.

A nature-loving outsider

Because of his Japanese heritage, David was often rejected by other Canadians of his own age. His lack of Japanese language skills saw to it, on the other hand, that he was punished with the scorn of his Japanese playmates. Out of this outsider situation, David early felt the desire to prove to everyone that he was ready for great things. This ambition, paired with his love of nature, became his driving force. After his exams as a geneticist, he was appointed as an assistant professor, and soon managed his own laboratory. David won the prestigious E.W.R. Steacie Memorial Scholarship, which is given to distinguished Canadian scientists under 35 years of age, in 1969. David's colleagues considered him an unconventional guy. He maintained friendly relationships with his students, openly stated his opinion in the face of opposition, and wore long hair and casual clothing. And yet, he made a very good reputation for himself in the scientific community.

The responsibility of the scientist

As a successful geneticist, David rose up on waves of the euphoria that were set in motion by the many innovations in gene technology. New techniques like DNA recombination, which made it possible to engender new traits in plants, animals and people, acted like drugs on most scientists. For the first time, people were in a position to make targeted changes to nature. At the time, David led a smooth-running laboratory with excellent scientists. All the hard work of past years seemed to be paying off.

But then the book *Silent Spring* by Rachel Carson, now a classic of the environmental movement, fell into his hands. He came across the following passage:

> You scientists are so intelligent, but you forget, that the laboratory is not the real world. In the real world, everything is linked to everything else. In the laboratory you run tests and these have special effects. In the real world, these experiments can provoke consequences in completely other areas, that no one realised before.

David admitted to us thoughtfully that – even now – these words overwhelmed him. They seemed to address him directly. His whole life long he had run down an educational path to become a scientist specialised in a narrow field. He had analysed certain genes in a certain type of fruit fly in order to understand what exactly was happening inside the fly and how that could eventually be altered. David slowly began to understand that this specialisation caused the biological big-picture to slip completely out of view. As he read Carson's book, it became clear to him how little geneticists thought about the possible consequences of their gene modifications. Who could know what effects a genetically altered plant growing not in the laboratory, but in the fields might have on the surrounding environment? What effects it might have on animals or people who eat it?

The meaning of genes

David often thinks back on his early childhood. When he was six years old, he was put into a prisoner of war camp with his family. The only reason for this was his Japanese national origin, his genes. At that time, during the Second World War, the assertions of geneticists about possible racial differences had terrible consequences for many millions of people. He had experienced with his own body what it was like to be beaten up by former friends, just because of a slight genetic difference. Regret, but also almost hate, describe his feelings best when, many years later, he became aware that universities did not cover the negative chapters of genetics with their students. In order to change this, David began to discuss the responsibilities of scientists publicly, much to the disapproval of his colleagues. Because he loved nature, he urged caution in the exposure of gene combinations whose effects in the wild were unknown.

Part of the problem or part of the solution?

David recognised that science, which he loved so much, was a part of the problem and not a part of the solution. He was completely convinced that only people who were very familiar with the subject matter and who were pursuing no special personal interests, could speak credibly about this topic. So he decided in 1978–9 to give up work in the laboratory and as a geneticist generally. He loved science, valued the work, and was active in an area that promised wealth and power. Yet David never regretted his decision. He had already learned early in his life from his father that the reason for living is not in order to pile up money and power. His father taught him to pity people who prided themselves on their big cars, their expensive clothes or other material luxuries. Money and power were not truly worth striving for. So David decided, after a difficult transition period, to follow his convictions. He remained active as a professor at the British Columbia University in Vancouver until he retired in 2001. In the years after that he devoted his energy to increasing responsibility in science and later in policy through information from scientists and the public.

And so, for more than 30 years, he has been moderating the documentary series *The Nature of Things*, in which he breaks down scientific discoveries and complex matters into understandable terms for millions of Canadians watching in their living rooms.

The time for solutions

A further turning point in David Suzuki's life was the period from 1988–1990. In 1988, he conducted 150 interviews with renowned scientists from various ecological disciplines in preparation for a radio series, *A Question of Survival*. David was surprised by the accumulating amount of bad news. Although he had already been intensively engaged for years in the earth's serious ecological problems, he thought to himself when he heard these conclusions, 'Dear God, the planet is being exposed to the attack of a powerful predator – people, and it will probably not survive this attack.' As the episodes were finally broadcast in 1990, he received 16,000 letters and almost all of them read similarly: 'We heard your programme, you filled us with an incredible fear, but what can just one person do?' His wife Tara then said, 'For years you've been telling people that we are in great difficulties. We have to show solutions and action.' David consulted with 15 other activists for three days. The group came to the decision that most organisations were founded in order to resolve a crisis. In this approach, problems lying at the root of the crisis remained untouched, rather what was attempted was merely getting the symptoms under control.

Yet as long as the destructive value system at the bottom of the problem of environmental devastation remained unchanged, short-term activism could help only little and less. For that reason, the group decided to establish the David Suzuki Foundation in 1990. Its purpose: to locate the underlying roots of human problems and to develop solutions and alternative actions on this basis. The solutions should rely on scientific analysis and address the 'masses'. When, on the publication of his book *Good News for Change*, he sent a copy to every member of the Canadian parliament and received no response, it was not the first time that he had had the sobering realisation that change would not occur from above. 'Most social leaders', according to David, 'would like circumstances to remain the same as they always were. They profit the most from that.' So, David began to pursue the goal of demonstrating to the everyday citizen what to do and why to do it.

A strategy for a future-ready Canada

Over the years, David developed more and more new approaches to solutions. At the beginning of the latest millennium, the idea came to him to look ahead one whole generation and use it as a brain-teaser: what would Canada look like in the year 2030, if everyone wanted to continue to enjoy the customary or possibly even higher quality of living? 'It was fairly easy', says David, 'to gather a consensus that the air in 2030 should be clean, the food edible and the running water drinkable.' Every Canadian could unite behind the goal of creating a Canada with a sustainable quality of living. The David Suzuki Foundation put together a document with the title *Sustainability in One Generation* in 2004. The question now was how to achieve the common goal. The foundation wanted to work out possibilities for penalising people who were against the goals of the plan. The results of this work process were recorded in the document *National Sustainability Development Strategy for Canada*, which the foundation published in 2006.

Grandchildren as motivation

When we asked David why he still undertakes all of these exertions at the age of 70, he replied:

My grandchildren give me the motivation. I won't rescue the world, and even my foundation won't be able to do this. But if there are a million people like me, who all do their best, and thousands of organisations like the David Suzuki Foundation, I believe that could be a significant force for good. At the end of my life, I want simply to be able to look into the eyes of my grandchildren and tell them reassuringly that grandpa did everything he could.

David admitted to us that he recognised 20 years ago that he could not save the world by himself. David can still remember exactly how it was when one day he looked in the mirror and said to himself: 'Who do you think you are? You think you are so important that you can save the world? Don't be so ego-centric, self-important and naive.' Since that day, David has felt as if a great burden has been lifted from his shoulders.

As David grows older, he has been asking himself, how he wants to be kept in people's memories. Smilingly, he said to us: 'I am like Fidel Castro. Fidel Castro said, the sun will burn out in about four billion years – who cares about the future?'

A glimpse into the future

David is certain that our species is condemned to ruin if we don't recognise our place on the earth, he told us:

Today most people think we are so clever that we don't need nature anymore. That is a huge tragedy. We don't know enough to manage the planet. We have to recognise again what true wealth is – community, family, the things that we do together, nature. I think if we can accept this again, we can be happier and less destructive creatures.

Information

- www.davidsuzuki.org
  Website of the David Suzuki Foundation.

- www.rightlivelihood.org/suzuki.html
  David Suzuki received the honorary lifetime Right Livelihood Award in 2009.

- Carson, R. (2007 [1962]) *Silent Spring* (New York: Houghton Mifflin Harcourt).

'By doing nothing, nothing can be left undone.'

Amory Lovins
Experimental physicist,
nature lover, photographer,
expert for resource efficiency
Snowmass, USA

Amory Lovins – Let's build a world: thriving, verdant, just and secure!

Amory Lovins was born in 1947, the son of an engineer and a social worker in Washington, DC. He didn't have an easy start in life. During his first ten years, he struggled with frequent infections of the respiratory tract due to a deficiency of red blood cells. His health condition was often so bad that he could not go to school for weeks on end. Fortunately, this did not bother the young bright boy too much. Amory had multiple interests and at home he could occupy himself with one of his favourite pastimes: reading. He did it so extensively that he left his fellow students far behind, which was not beneficial when it came to socialising with his peers. Who wants to spend time with a boy who is making a living as a physics consultant at the age of 15, leaves the impression that he already holds a degree in mathematics, chemistry and other natural sciences, is an excellent musician, profoundly literate in the classics and a half-professional photographer?

Academic island-hopping

At the age of 16, Amory got the chance to transfer to the elite university Harvard and leave his school days in Amherst, Massachusetts behind. Because he had a Nobel Prize winner as a physics teacher, Harvard was able to fascinate the young genius for a short period of time. However, he didn't want to specialise at such an early age. In our conversation with Amory in 2006 he explained to us that learning knowledge that is interdependent and interconnected in isolation is not only senseless, but harmful. So Amory went to Oxford in Great Britain at the age of 18 because there he was able to experiment and study in a more interdisciplinary way. 'I wasn't just an empty vessel that you could fill up with facts,' he told us, with a glint of rebellion in his eyes. When the money Amory had earned as a physics consultant ran low, his Indian squash partner advised him to apply for a scholarship. It was not until during his interview that he realised he had confused the forms and instead of applying for support for a half-year term, he was now in the running for a three-year research stipend at Merton College, one of England's best schools. People who knew him, however, were not surprised that he was credited with this special opportunity and consequently was able to delve deeply into biophysics, while maintaining his other interests.

The real problems and part of the solution

After two years of concentrated research, the young scientist concluded that all of the serious problems calling for solutions in this world are connected to energy and natural resources. In 1971, however, neither Merton College nor any other place on earth was able to offer him the opportunity to do research and write a dissertation on the topic of energy management. This was two years after the worldwide oil crisis and decades before climate change, the limits of fossil fuel sources and the destruction of natural resources became broadly discussed topics. So again, Amory decided to quit his studies, against the well-intentioned advice of professors and colleagues. 'If you are not part of the solution, you are part of the problem!' This saying of the African-American activist Carmichael had deeply impressed him, and he felt like he could no longer justify standing around in a lab for additional years. While academic work was fascinating to him, it was not enabling him to make any real contribution with regard to the energy and resource problems facing the world.

In 1971, the academic world was not concerned with these problems, so Amory started his own consulting firm at the age of 24. His firm concentrated on advising large energy corporations and private enterprises that seriously wanted to do something about the world's energy problems. Amory was con-vinced – much to the dismay of many followers of the ecological movement – that instead of activism, consultation with international corporations was a more effective way to bring about positive change. This was the 1970s, when activism had appeal and corporations did not.

Heating a house with sun and body heat at 2,200 metres?

Demanding and exciting consulting projects around the world set the tenor for Amory's next ten years in London. Europe was an interesting base for his work, because the debate about energy politics was more advanced there at that time than anywhere else in the world.

It was about then when the young, multi-talented man read a monograph about wildlife protection, and came into contact with the environmental organisation Friends of the Earth. Later he became their representative in Europe. Since he was commissioned with the publication of several land-scape photography books, he was also able to live out his passion for moun-tain climbing, hiking and photography during this time.

After his marriage in 1979, Amory wanted to return to the USA, and after a short stay in Los Angeles he decided to found the Rocky Mountain Institute (RMI), together with his wife Hunter, in Snowmass, Colorado. This is where we wet met Amory in the middle of winter. The institute lies at a height of 2,220 metres above sea level, far from the tourist-crowded skiing regions around

Aspen. From the beginning, this impressive building was conceptualised as an example of resource-friendly construction. Cosy, thick stone walls guarantee good insulation and the water is branched off from a nearby source. A winter garden captures all the sun rays that make their way down to this cold region. The house is heated by solar energy and body warmth. Besides its exemplary energy balance, a very comfortable atmosphere characterises the resource-passive building.

Press-ready words

This atmosphere matches Amory's amiable aura. He is a man of medium height with a friendly face and vivid eyes. As we arrived at the RMI, he had just ended a conference call. He asked us where we came from and greeted us in German. He told us that he cannot say much more than *Guten Tag* in our language, but he pulled a Bavarian mug from his kitchen pantry and filled it with clear mountain water. To show all his guests attention and make them happy, he also showed us the Polish version of a book on sustainability published by the Club of Rome. We wondered, 'does he have something in stock for every nationality?'

We began an exciting conversation that was interrupted several times by the phone. Amory answered some of the calls and we are amazed how he was able to seamlessly continue each sentence exactly where he left it after an interruption. All the time he was completely present in our conversation. His answers were well thought through and perfectly formulated.

Affluence by design

First, Amory recalled the beginnings of RMI. Back in the 1980s, Amory and Hunter Lovins gathered a group of colleagues in Snowmass in order to realise the mission of RMI as effectively as possible. This mission, grown out of experience, is in place to this day: 'To drive the efficient and restorative use of resources in order to build a world thriving, verdant and secure, for all, forever!' In short: to create affluence through intelligent design.

Aside from innumerable publications and presentations that have originated within a working group of experts at RMI, the team of 50 people has developed innovative solutions in 50 different countries and in 22 different industry sectors in the last years. In the US alone, RMI has supported 80 of the Fortune 500 companies – the biggest corporations – in sectors as disparate as the chemical industry, computer chip production and retail. As a prerequisite for cooperation, the management needs to be sufficiently receptive to new ideas. Often Amory and his colleagues aim to work towards change within two leading enterprises within the same branch. That way, these companies serve as role models and successful exemplars, motivating other enterprises of the same branch to make similar adjustments. The team quickly moves on to the next industry sector after that, because, as Amory explained to us, 'If we are to successfully transform our systems before it is too late, a lot must yet be done.' Besides consulting with private corporations, RMI also supports governments in important future-oriented questions. RMI's last book, *Winning the Oil Endgame*, for instance, was written for the Pentagon. Amory works with the military on diverse initiatives today in order to end the USA's dependence on oil within the next decades. He claims that the priorities of RMI are relatively void of ideology, but it is very clear: first, save the world; second, have fun doing it; third, make money – exactly in that order.

Constantly walking the tightrope

To his critics, who accuse him of getting into bed with the 'enemy' because he is working with large corporations, he replies with a wink: 'By doing nothing, nothing can be left undone.'

He is an optimist who believes in the future of the 'human experiment'. He wants to serve with his talent and his work by finding solutions: solutions that bring about systems that make the world more thriving, verdant, just and secure. That is why Amory invests his energy into areas that he thinks show the biggest necessity for change, but due to their position, they also have the greatest impact on overall developments. In the last few years, he has spent a lot of time advocating for change in the CO_2-based automobile industry. He has developed innovative solutions for the construction industry, the semiconductor industry, the water industry and the energy industry. Amory helped these and other industry branches to use natural resources more efficiently, or at least differently.

> There are three main sectors that can change society: the public sector, civil society – mostly represented by non-governmental organisations – and the private sector. They are more likely to follow our advice if they pay for it than if we give it to them. Therefore, we mainly work in this last sector. Some people say that we are working with the enemy. It's a balancing act, as you change things. It's okay if they have done bad things in the past, as long as they sincerely want to change at a sufficiently senior level to make it happen.

As an example, RMI recently achieved a massive reduction of CO_2 emissions with Wal-Mart – one of the most infamous retail corporations worldwide. Consequently, the delivery fleet alone has reduced its emissions by half.

Dancing with a stronger partner

Sometimes Amory is frustrated, because he is presenting solutions today that he already published 25 years ago in almost the exact same form. It's just that back then nobody was willing to listen. Without acrimony, he recalls:

> Just the other day I was reading an article I wrote in 1980 which – if followed – would have resulted in aborting practically all the pro-liferation of nuclear weapons that we've had since then. So . . . in a way you can hold those who did not follow that advice morally responsible. But if we think of them as bad people – how is this helpful to changing our behaviour today? I think it's still construc-tive to do what we tried to do then, namely to say: 'You can achieve your objectives much better by doing things in a different way'. It's like in Aikido, the non-violent martial art: you dance with a partner. You are committed to process an outcome in the belief that from a good process will emerge a much better outcome than anyone had in mind initially.

Today, Amory also knows that most industry sectors are subject to very long cycles of change. These cycles take about 30 years in the automobile sector and 50 years in the energy sector.

However, it is necessary to permanently work on innovative solutions, so that these can be implemented at the right time. Even if this requires some patience, it is deeply satisfying for Amory to move forward a small step every day. He knows that he is working on the right topics – topics that are part of a process leading to a better world.

The human experiment

Amory has fun learning new things and he enjoys working towards solutions to relevant problems, surrounded by inspiring personalities. There is almost nothing more beautiful for him than influencing the way people think about fundamental problems and thereby creating fundamental change. For him it is unquestionable that he will always care for the future of humankind. 'It's just who I am, sorry.'

He thinks it is too early to say whether or not the 'experiment of human-kind' really was a good idea. As he said to us, eventually, we are still on our way to becoming higher primates. The experimental physicist wants to make his contribution to this process. Amory thinks that we all have the responsi-bility to recast our projects and machines for a better future:

> Fortunately we know in the whole universe there is nothing more powerful than six billion human brains, which are striving to solve a problem. And these brains are evenly distributed – one per person.

Become a better person on the journey

'If there are people who want to use this life opportunity to play video games, that's their business. But that's not who I am.' Amory hopes that he will vastly improve the well-being of people with his activities. With his team of system analysts, he is looking for ways to better implement the mission of RMI every day. This world shall become more just, secure thriving and verdant – a vision that Amory has been following for over 25 years now, regardless of whether it was actually popular or not the right time. Using resources wisely is a rule for the way, but it is not the ultimate goal:

> We are trying to create a world that takes nothing, wastes nothing and does no harm. And I would also hope that besides the technological improvements that achieve a well-designed balance, we would simply develop a clearer idea of what life is truly worth in the world. And we are moving towards a fairer and safer world, which is much more stringent on resource efficiency. Along the way, through all my interactions I hope to become a better human being whom others support.

Information

- www.rmi.org
  Website of the Rocky Mountain Institute.

- www.naturalcapitalism.org
  Website of the book Natural Capitalism.

- www.smallisprofitable.org
  Website of the book Small is Profitable: The Hidden Economic Benefits of Making Electrical Resources the Right Size.

- www.rmi.org/ReinventingFire
  Website of the book Reinventing Fire: Bold Business Solutions for the New Energy Era.

'Very few people can actually treat an adult as an adult. I treat everyone in my company as an adult.'

Charles Maisel
Economist, entrepreneur, artist, fighter for the disadvantaged
Cape Town, South Africa

Charles Maisel – Treat adults as adults

Hidden between warehouses, about 20 minutes from the centre of Cape Town, we found the headquarters of Men at the Side of the Road (MSR). 'Unfortunately, Charles is not here. He was called to a government secretary this morning to discuss an important issue,' apologised Jocelyne, Charles Maisel's wife. Jocelyne, who mostly helps her husband with organisation and planning, showed us the centrepiece of MSR: rooms full of used tools – hammers, pliers, shovels, lawn mowers, gardening rakes and utensils for painting. It offered an unusual sight and it took us some time to see the connection to social development. The tools we saw were donated by volunteers from all over South Africa and partially from abroad. MSR makes detailed efforts to repair these tools and sells or lends them to the many thousand men in Cape Town living on the poverty line. Thanks to the tools, they can earn at least enough money as gardeners, masons or painters to sustain their families.

Men at the Side of the Road

There are 500 places across Cape Town where day labourers wait for the opportunity to work. Their numbers are estimated at around 50,000. One day, Charles Maisel began talking to these men. They told him that they were often treated and paid poorly, didn't even have the most basic sanitary facilities at their disposal and could do absolutely nothing about the miserable conditions.

It didn't take Charles very long to develop a plan. Within two years, the organisation MSR came to life. It gives these workers a voice in society, helps them to get organised and support one another. Many employers pay their workers lower wages than originally agreed on. Sometimes they abandon workers at sites that lie hundreds of kilometres away from Cape Town because the transportation that workers were promised was never arranged. Not to mention working conditions: many men do not even want to talk about them because they feel ashamed.

After the first successful outcomes, Charles shifted into full gear. He organised the construction of stands that provided shade to those waiting for work and he established sanitary facilities. Soon he noticed that the men were able to earn more money if they had better training, so he organised training for painters, craftsmen and gardeners. However, having had many years of experience with disenfranchised people who were fighting just to get by every day, he knew that free training was not enough. Transport to the training site and back home had to be covered, and the men and their families had to be sustained so that they could concentrate on their vocational training. So Charles Maisel signed cooperation agreements with the South African government, which is now supporting the programmes as preparation for the job market.

Since education is not enough to get a job in South Africa, Charles added two more elements to his model. It became clear to him that it would be much better for the workers if they had their own tools and even their own contracts. However, he also knew that they could never afford new tools and also did not have the contacts or credibility to get contracts. At the same time, many of Charles's friends had unused or broken tools lying in their garages. It made sense to organise a campaign to collect and repair them. Subsequently, 20,000 tools have been gathered through further collection campaigns that were also conducted abroad. MSR is currently repairing, storing and lending out these tools at five locations in South Africa. In addition, MSR also started an agency so that workers could have better access to suitable jobs.

Meanwhile, the agency has grown to be one of the largest in South Africa and mostly offers men contact with small-scale jobs in the areas of gardening, painting and crafts of all kinds. But who is the man behind all these ideas? How does he think? And what motivates him?

The unorthodox leadership of an artist

Two days later, as we met Charles in a café in one of Cape Town's suburbs we couldn't stop smiling at his words. Every sentence this man says would shake the very foundations of European and American business beliefs. He sat in front of us in comfortable clothes with a wool hat and told us:

> My imagination is simple: I do not work for corporate enterprises. I do not work for materialistic purposes and I never have. I'm an economist, I was trained as an economist at university, but I've never worked as an economist. I don't work for money. Why not? I don't think a good enough imagination is worth it. If you work based on your passion, then you create what I call 'art'. It doesn't matter if you're an accountant, a doctor, a lawyer, or an economist like me – you can create art in any field. If you're just working for the sake of earning your pay cheque then your project's just going to be meaningless.

If you want to learn a certain profession, Charles thinks school and apprenticeships are not the way. Charles proposes shadowing and working with a person who is performing at a very high professional level and does his or her job with love.

> When you get the point of being an artist then what you do leads you to the top of your game. It leads you to creating stuff that's unique and fresh and alive. People look at it and they say 'Wow!' they can connect with it . . .

Working for Charles is a very different experience,

... there are no time constraints, there is no leave policy, no job description and no rules, not one, because there are no rules for creating an environment where people can grow. There are no salaries, if you want to work for me you tell me what you want to make, and if I really want you then I'll just accept it, that's it. You don't write reports for my projects and we don't have meetings. If there is trouble, they can come to me and we'll have a dialogue.

Charles's origin was a lot less revolutionary than his views are today. He comes from a wealthy South African family. He had the privilege to go to a very good school and then to study economics at an elite university. After he graduated with a good degree, he had to serve in the military for two years. After that he wanted to see more of the world and travelled in Europe for a year. In 1992, he returned to South Africa and began his work as a creative problem solver or an 'artist' as he calls himself.

I don't have a niche. I don't believe that I'm the unemployment specialist or that I'm the domestic violence specialist or the AIDS specialist. I do hundreds of projects on all different things; I just find a different way to do them, that's all. The MSR project is probably going to be the biggest unemployment project in the whole country. But I can't sell it like a businessman, I can give it away. That's what I do with my projects. I don't get any money and I don't want to manage a project forever.

Since Charles does not like to be dependent on donations and wants his creations to outlive him for a long time, the economic aspect of his initiatives is very important to him. Therefore he tries to shape projects so that they can sustain themselves. He claimed to us that this is quite easy:

A good businessman with a clear mind sees a gap in society and fills it. My gaps are more social in nature. I'll see big gaps around themes, like unemployment or AIDS or violence and then I design creative models around those themes. My skill is to fill those gaps. I'm a marketer. My models are different; a very high percentage of them will carry on. I hand pick the people who I think can do this.

And with regard to MSR, Charles said:

Tools are only a small part of it. It was more important to give these people a voice, a mechanism so that they can speak for themselves and others don't have to speak for them. Now, we run our own businesses from here. We do gardening, landscaping and construction. This is probably going to be the biggest unemployment project in the next three years in the whole country. There also are two new projects that I really like. One is that we are designing furniture for the average 16 square-metre house in the poor areas. Usually about five or six people are sleeping in these four by fours. The other project we're doing is called the African Overalls. You know the ones that you wear in the factories are usually grey or blue. We are designing one with colourful African print that we want to sell all over the world.

In spite of these great developments, Charles told us that he was about to say goodbye to MSR. He said that the project was running capably and that he is just not the type of person for management issues. In his mind, his next project had already been born. Therefore, he wanted to give MSR to the people who had helped him build up the venture over the years, and who had proven themselves to be capable managers. To ask for financial compensation, as is common in the business world, was out of the question for Charles. What was important to him was that an important problem was solved with the help of his talent, and that the solution can sustain itself in the future.

Trading ideas the Maisel way

The new company Charles has in mind will be called The Great Ideas Company. Charles wants to solve the problem that many good ideas are never realised. The concept he is designing is based on a mobile phone platform through which he is planning to buy millions of ideas before he begins trading with these ideas. The technology of choice is the mobile phone because more people in Africa have access to mobile phones than the Internet. In recent years he had already received ideas via SMS, purchased them from the originator, and sold them to people whom he knew were capable of and interested in realising these ideas.

Overall, this idea seems no less out-of-the-box than collecting old tools. But Charles is optimistic and explained to us that no one so far has even tried to trade with ideas – let alone ideas that are too risky for investors and banks. His most important target group is young people. They are so creative and innovative, he believes that he will soon have an enormous repertoire of ideas.

Room for personal growth

We asked Charles why he never thinks about the financial security of a salary or the opinion of others when he works. He explained:

> I've always been like this. I come from a wealthy background. Because I've won all these international awards, my family is proud now. But if I hadn't, and I hadn't gone through school then maybe they wouldn't be. It's too difficult for people to understand people like me because they think that you have to pay school fees so you can put bread on the table. For me, that all can come quite easily if your passion is your art. How could you ever tell a painter,

a writer or whatever to stop doing what they are doing because they aren't making a living? You can't, and I think that should be the same in every profession. Do you know what the biggest disease in this world is? Depression, why? Because people are not doing what they really want.

Once again, Charles stressed the importance of empowering workers:

I think the difference between a mature artist and an immature artist is that the former can treat everyone as an adult. It sometimes is very difficult, especially in the work environment. Very few people can actually treat an adult as an adult. I treat everyone in my company as an adult. I am not their father or mother. They pick that up quick. Not one person has left my projects, ever–unless they got a promotion elsewhere. They need space to grow and I create the space for that. You can't take people for granted.

Information

- 12businesses.blogspot.ch
  Charles Maisel's blog on starting 12 businesses in 12 months.

'Selling cars, computers or metal pipes would just not be enough for me – I want to make the world a better place.'

Thilo Bode
Foreign aid worker,
environmentalist,
entrepreneur, agent of
change
Berlin, Germany

Thilo Bode – Change in the face of opposition

We knew Thilo Bode from the press, from newspaper reports about Greenpeace activists who chained themselves to whaling fleets and oil platforms. This was in the early 1990s. We later heard his name in connection with the Kyoto protocol, the discussion on the ozone layer and the scandal surrounding the Shell platform, Brent Spar. These matters, however, all lay in the past.

We wondered, what happens when you are no longer an environmental activist – or is it that you actually stay one forever? What is life like if you are the former director of Greenpeace International and how do you even get a job like that?

We had the chance to ask questions such as these in the meeting room of Foodwatch, the new organisation founded by Thilo Bode when we met. Underlining the start-up character of Foodwatch, the offices were tucked away in one of Berlin's many rear buildings, where Mr Bode was still busy making financial plans for the next board meeting.

At almost 60 years of age, he had greeted us with a relaxed smile. He had heard that we wanted to talk to people who were making positive contributions to the world, but he was quick to redefine the course of our conversation: individuals, he said modestly, tend to overestimate their own contributions and change only happens with the help of strong teams. In addition, he told us, contributions are only effective when the right moment, the right place and the right abilities come together. This promised to be an interesting exchange.

Rebellion and the politics of youth

Thilo Bode grew up in a conservative household in Ammersee, Bavaria. Thus, he had already had some practice in implementing change in the face of opposition. As a young man he was already fascinated by the origins of social injustice and the possibilities for mitigating it. Where his interest in these topics developed cannot be determined exactly, but perhaps it was simply the spirit of his age. Whatever the case, he was programmed from the beginning to improve the world. He founded a local group of the Young Social Democrats within the German Social Democratic Party and ascended the political ladder until he became head of a district. However, after five years of political activity, he noticed that there are many systemic forces that limit the effectiveness of party politics and consequently real changes can only partially be initiated in the political sphere. Nevertheless, he enjoyed being politically active during his college years in Munich and Regensburg, where he studied sociology and economics. Many discussions, however, remained theoretical, which is why he decided to go into foreign aid after he had graduated with a

PhD focused on direct investments in Asia in 1975. He believed that here he would be able to put into practice all that he had read over the past years.

Structural deficits in foreign aid

What followed were 12 years of foreign aid work in many developing countries for the Credit Institution for Reconstruction (Kreditanstalt für Wiederaufbau, KfW). Bode planned, financed and implemented water supply and energy projects until he came to a point at which he became disillusioned with foreign aid work. As he told us, the type of foreign aid that used to be common back then was problematic in many ways. The troubles were seldom of a financial or educational nature but, rather, they were the result of massive structural and organisational deficits. The basic philosophy of foreign aid has widely changed over the last years, but back then this was not yet the case.

Difficult conditions for enterprises

After more than ten years working in foreign aid, Thilo Bode also wanted to gain some first-hand experience in the industrial sector. He applied for a position as a management assistant in a mid-sized enterprise in metal processing. Bode assured us that he learned a lot during his three years there. He developed high respect for mid-sized enterprises that are led by their owners. In contrast to top managers of global corporations who often get high rewards for questionable performances, smaller entrepreneurs deserve admiration. They struggle with difficult conditions imposed from outside and they have little say in policy affairs. Through his work in the industrial sector, Bode learned to understand how entrepreneurs think and which pressures they are exposed to. This understanding helped him in many of the arguments he had during his career and it often earned him the respect of the other side. Anyone who plans on saving the world by working for an NGO would do well to work for a company for a while as preparation, said Bode. He did not himself want to spend his life selling things: 'Selling cars, computers or metal pipes may be exciting for some – but it did not make me happy.' He wanted to invest his energy into bringing justice to the world.

Greenpeace: Change through NGOs?

Thilo Bode was already mentally preparing to leave the enterprise when he saw an announcement by Greenpeace in the paper. A new director for Germany was being sought. He did not believe he had a good chance of getting the position, but the job seemed to offer exciting challenges that allowed for a real contribution to change. So he filed an application and, to his surprise, got the job. From the beginning, he made one basic demand: he wanted to reserve the right to make unpopular decisions. This wish was granted, albeit through gritted teeth, and that is how, in 1989, a close and successful 12-year relationship began between Bode and Greenpeace. Looking back, Bode thinks that he simply was the right man, at the right time, in the right place to make the necessary changes at Greenpeace. He worked on this on a national level and later, as of 1995, on an international level after he became director of Greenpeace International.

When Thilo Bode first came to Greenpeace the organisation had seen a period of rapid growth. It had developed into an internationally-renowned environmental organisation and gained much influence and popularity. However, flaws in both the organisation and in its leadership were increasing – a typical development during growth. Bode's rich professional experience made an excellent contribution here. As a politically-minded person with good economic expertise, he was able to lead Greenpeace into an era of success. At first, he wasn't completely sure what he was letting himself in for:

> I didn't join Greenpeace with a fixed notion or vision of what people should be doing rather, I had the courage to listen to people. In the years that followed these discussions, a new direction and vision was born. Before you can change anything efficiently, you have to understand the weaknesses and abilities of an organisation.

This process was not always easy, but it led to success. These were the years of the first major eco-political breakthroughs. The Montreal agreement on protection of the ozone layer, the convention on biodiversity conservation and the Kyoto protocol were all signed in this year. Greenpeace always played a part and became the vanguard of the environmental lobby.

Following the urge to change

Bode enjoyed entering controversial negotiations with 'the bad' on the side of 'the good'. But in 2001, despite the success he had achieved, it was his gut feeling that he had to leave Greenpeace if he wanted to continue his path. In his opinion, the organisation was not ready for further change, which was partly due to its history of success. The logical conclusion for Bode was to step down – a decision not everyone around him could understand. At the time he did not know what the next step would be. He told us that he can now see that in every change there also is a risk, but back then he was not as aware of it and he would not have been content if he hadn't taken that step.

Over the years, Thilo Bode has increasingly realised that change through politics and enterprises is very limited, since all activities are always bound to a system. He explained to us: 'Organisations like that are meant to stabilise, not change things. If you want to change things you need to join an organisation that makes change its goal!'

An erosion of democracy

A time of reorientation followed. Bode was asked by a publisher whether or not he would like to write a book. He did not want to write a book about the internal life of Greenpeace – which was an obvious suggestion. But he could imagine writing about something that increasingly caught his attention: 'I came to the conclusion that we were currently experiencing an erosion of democracy in favour of strong interest groups and to the disadvantage of the common good.' In his book *Democracy is Betraying Its Children* he shows how national and international politics, as well as economic conditions, are influenced by strong lobbies that can practically no longer be controlled by citizens. However, during his Greenpeace years, he repeatedly had the experience that people can exert a strong influence if they unite and follow a common goal. According to Bode, we have more influence than we think: 'The masquerade of politics for status and interest quickly crumbles, if we organise.' In his experience alone, consumers are like dwarfs, but 'together they are a giant'.

Food and the power of consumers

While working as an author, Bode also founded Foodwatch. The aim of Foodwatch is to represent the interests of consumers in the food sector and also to increase its democratic control. The politically independent organisation is financed by membership fees and donations. This is the only way to remain independent with regard to its activist agenda. The Foodwatch team now consists of ten members, who avidly advocate market transparency, safe nutrition and consumer protection. Membership is directed towards people who care about their health as well as the social and global effects of their behaviour as buyers. Foodwatch counted 17,000 supporters in 2010.

According to Foodwatch, consumers should have the right to know what the food products they buy for themselves and their family contain. The industry should take responsibility for its products and face stronger regulation. The summarised mission statement on the organisation's website reads: 'Foodwatch makes things clear: we do independent research and analysis, we tell the public which food products contain toxins, we name the parties responsible and we tell consumers about the barefaced lies used in food advertising.'

Clear legislation and the consequential implementation of laws in the interest of consumers is certainly part of Foodwatch's mission. Democracy will return to the food sector. Thilo Bode explained the connection to us:

> It is not easy to explain to people, that there is a deficit of democracy in the food sector – there is hardly any transparency, no real freedom of choice and hardly any protection. Since the media is reporting less and less critically, there is little possibility to exert control. I see Foodwatch as a symbol for democracy. I want to make clear to people that they must actively unite to make change happen.

In the meantime, the organisation has become well-established, has launched several campaigns drawing public attention and has been invited for consultations by the press and politicians. The rotten meat scandal in Germany and similar events are clear indicators that organisations like Foodwatch are needed.

At the end of our meeting, Thilo Bode wrapped up his experience as a professional 'agent of change':

> Social problems, especially social injustice, always interested me. Back in the day, I got engaged in party politics, after that I worked in foreign aid and in the industrial sector. Finally, I realised that the most efficient way to make change happen lies in uniting individual interests.

Information

- foodwatch.de/english/index_ger.html

  Foodwatch informs the public about the quality of food products and defends the rights of consumers through campaigns and independent research as well as at court.

- www.greenpeace.org

'The loss of connection to our inner self, the people around us and especially with nature is a root problem of our time.'

Junko Edahiro
Translator, source of
information, agent of change,
fountain of hope
Tokyo, Japan

Junko Edahiro – Fountain of hope in critical times

We came across Junko Edahiro and her projects through a simple Google search. 'Japan' and 'sustainability' gave us the predictable result, 'Japan for sustainability', which is the name of Junko's organisation. It has the aim of informing the world of Japan's progress in the areas of environmental protection and sustainability. A clear mission statement – and easy to find.

In the second half of 2005, we met Junko in her quaint and simple office located in a quiet part of Tokyo. It is situated in a neighbourhood with a bit of green here and there, and the chirp of birds can even be heard once in a while – very unusual in the artificial and sterile environment of this enormous metropolis, which is densely populated with 35 million inhabitants.

We were politely asked to take off our shoes, as is the custom in Japan. Then we stepped into a room, the walls of which were covered with plain, but comfortable cork tiles and bookshelves. Checking the spines of the books didn't really leave us knowing more about her than we had already learned. Almost everything was in Japanese. But a few English books by Lester Brown[20] were familiar. How they got there would soon be explained to us.

An ordinary Japanese girl

Junko Edahiro speaks perfect English, and her face carries a serious, concentrated expression. In the first 30 years of her life nothing pointed towards a future concerned with environment and sustainability – let alone English. Junko grew up in Tokyo, went to one of the schools there, got married early and graduated from the University of Tokyo with a master of arts degree in educational psychology. Despite her aversion to foreign languages, she decided to go to the USA with her husband, who was commencing studies at the famous Princeton University. Up until the age of 29, Junko's life was quite typical for a Japanese woman – she had been brought up and educated well and eventually focused on supporting her husband and her family. With regard to the preconceptions that exist towards Japanese students, it was less typical that she learned English perfectly well within only two years. Her English was so good that she was able to work as an interpreter.

Junko had always been interested in literature. So she began translating books from English into Japanese while she was in the USA. In the beginning, she touched on many different subjects with her work. But over time, she focused more and more on ecological topics. Unexpectedly, Junko had found an area that was appealing and fascinating to her.

---

20 Lester Brown was the founder of the Worldwatch Institute and of the Earth Policy Institute, two of the most important think-tanks of the ecological movement worldwide.

Growing interest

On her return to Japan, Junko learned about the ideas of Lester Brown, one of the legends of the environmentalist movement. She got to know him personally when she became the interpreter of his presentations and conversations during his tour through Japan. Her dedication to the environmental cause consequently increased. His conversations often revolved around questions of how to create a system of worldwide sustainability, and were both an inspiration and an unbelievably rich source of knowledge. Owing to a small innovation, Junko multiplied her working speed: she dictated her translations onto tapes and then had them typed up. In this manner, she translated about 20 books into Japanese in the following years, including almost all of Lester Brown's publications. Translating was, however, only the beginning of her journey. Soon the young woman published her own book on sustainability. Even though it was a heart-felt endeavour to her, it did not receive a lot of public attention.

Get up at two in the morning and you can do it all!

Junko became a mother shortly after that. However, this did not mark the end of her career as is unfortunately still the case for so many women in Japan. Instead, becoming a mother was the reason for her most successful book so far: *Get up at Two in the Morning and You Can Do It All!* When she put her daughter to bed at eight in the evening, she started going to sleep with her. And since Junko only needs about six hours of sleep, she took advantage of the new rhythm and got up at two in the morning. After she realised how productive the time between two and nine in the morning was – undisturbed by phone calls and email – she wrote a much-read book about it. She also included the topic of sustainability. The trick worked.

Not that ecologically backward

Proud of her bestselling book and still highly interested in the ecological topics of our time, Junko's success rate accelerated in the years that followed. In 1999, she started an email newsletter in which she compiled the most interesting and important news on sustainability that she had read and heard about Japan at different conventions. She noticed that Japan was ecologically not as backward as first impressions made it seem. The initial 18 people who showed interest in her work became over 8,000 subscribers from Japan and abroad over the course of a few years. In 2002, Junko therefore decided to establish a permanent news platform under the name Japan for Sustainability.

However, she didn't try doing this alone. Instead, she organised an innovative system of 350 volunteers who now hold responsibilities in areas such as editing, proofing and publishing. Together they contribute enough so that the platform can publish around 30, high-quality articles every month.

Junko explained to us:

> The basis of my work is not that I am against something, but rather I am for something. I want to support constructive dialogue. That is why my cooperation with partners from various enterprises and also public administration is so successful.

In practice, this means that she and her team report on the positive activities of Japanese companies, the Japanese state and individual citizens in the area of sustainability. There is no time for charges and accusations. In addition, her experience in Japan has shown that when people actively contribute their own information to the organisation's work, the more valuable, highly informative news they receive. That means that whenever Junko sends out her news messages, she receives a large amount of invaluable information back: not only hints on new products and projects, solutions and initiatives, but also feedback on new trends from individual areas.

The journey is the destination

Junko told us that there were no specific, outstanding or transforming events in her life and no extraordinary experiences that led her to become seriously dedicated to sustainability issues. It was something that unfolded slowly and grew stronger over time. She was specifically concerned because of the large number of people who are pessimistic about the future of our planet. Junko admitted that she is not at all sure whether humanity has a chance of survival. What she is sure of is that she will do everything within her power to increase that chance. During our meeting, Junko made a determined, but open-minded impression. She seemed relaxed, but at the same time conveyed a certain urgency. The simple way she wore her hair and her serious, but friendly face underlined this twofold impression.

Junko wants to be a source of hope for others in an environment that she thinks will become increasingly difficult and pessimistic. She confirmed something we have heard several times with other leading figures in the ecological movement: it is crucial to be conscious of the fact that you are contributing something positive. This realisation provides satisfaction and energy on a daily basis – so much, in fact, that merely selfish motives would suffice for making a positive contribution.

The biggest problem today: A lack of connectivity

Junko thinks that the loss of connectivity is one of the basic problems of our time. The loss of connection with ourselves, with those around us and especially with nature, leads to a situation in which many of our daily activities are harmful for us. We often live as if we are moving through a space void of interconnections. For instance, as if our economic activities have no relationship with the destruction of the environment and its effect on us, and as if the money that flows from the great stock exchanges around the world does not have real effects on the lives of many people.

Junko feels that many of us have also lost connection with ourselves, and that we often do not know anymore what is good for us and where the limits of work and consumption are exceeded. The lack of connection with nature is responsible for our thoughtless and unconcerned destruction of it. We have lost the awareness that we are destroying the basis of our lives. And finally, the loss of connection to other human beings leads us to ignore that 1.2 billion people do not have access to clean water and that 30,000 people die of curable diseases every day. At the same time, unbelievable amounts of money are invested in destructive weapon arsenals. This lack of awareness of the interdependences of things is one of today's main problems, according to Junko. She believes that we are at a turning point in history: it is time to restore these connections.

New activities and plans

Junko has called for action on many different occasions. She calls on other people to act and supports them in it. In 2003, for instance, she initiated the 'Candle Night' together with the movement Slow Life. Since then, about five million Japanese citizens follow her call twice a year and congregate at night under the free sky, simply to spend a few quiet hours in the light of their candles.

Junko's other initiatives include Eco Networks, Change Agent and e's, which stands for: ecology, empowerment, energy, enthusiasm and Edahiro. The latter organisation sells eco-products and offers courses for Japanese women supporting them as they make changes in their careers and lifestyles. What they learn is not meant to contribute only to a personal change, but also encourage the women to initiate processes of change in their communities and in society.

Eco Networks offers translations and consulting services for Japanese companies in the field of communication. The focus here lies on corporate social responsibility and sustainability. The organisation Change Agent takes things a step further. The aim is to train agents of change at a higher level. With the help of insights from system theory and system modelling, people are supposed to be enabled to induce changes in Japan on a large scale. Participants learn about theories and methods and are integrated in suitable networks. One of Junko's newest initiatives is the web platform, 'Children for the Future'. With its help she wants to educate the upcoming generation with regard to sustainability, so that her successful work will hopefully last.

Positive impact and a fountain of hope

Having success does not mean acquiring more money, power and fame for Junko Edahiro. She measures success with regard to its effect on a more sustainable way of living. For Junko, progress means to move the world into a direction in which our consumption of resources – or our ecological footprint as Mathis Wackernagel[21] calls it – makes long-term survival of humankind possible. The fame she has acquired through her books and seminars is meaningless, she said to us, if they do not lead to real change in the world.

With all her activities, Junko wants to create a more liveable and sustainable world as well as be a role model for other Japanese women who still hesitate to become active in an area of their choice because they are afraid of societal pressures and the disapproval of others. Junko wants to show them that they can develop freely, even if this implies not fulfilling all external expectations.

And, even though Junko's children are too old now to go sleep with her, she still gets up at two o'clock in the morning:

> In the coming years, there will be some overwhelming and dramatic developments in the world. In this negative atmosphere, people will give up and despair. But I believe in the power of positive information and I want to provide a fountain of hope. And in this regard, I really hope that your book will have a positive impact on the lives of other people.

---

21 Mathis Wackernagel is the founder and manager of the non-profit organisation, Global Footprint Network. In order to evaluate the ecological footprint of people, their use of resources is documented and converted into the surface on earth that is necessary to provide the respective resources. This shows how much space a person or a region is using, or in other words, how many planets we would need if all the people on earth had the same consumption rate as the developed world.

Information

- www.japanfs.org

  Japanese platform for sustainability on which Junko Edahiro and 350 volunteers are publishing everything worth knowing about sustainability in Japan.

- www.es-inc.jp

  e's is a company that Junko Edahiro founded in 2004 in order to support people who wish to undergo personal change.

- www.candle-night.org

  Website about the Candle Night.

- www.change-agent.jp

  Change Agent trains people to become agents of change.

CONCLUSION

Five insights and experiences from Chapter 5:

1. It is important to find your own path and not to live the life that others consider good for you

2. Discovering this path often sets free unexpected potential and energy. To live according to your calling, is a joyful and satisfying experience

3. It takes courage and self-confidence to endure the disapproval and scepticism of your environment. But if you stay true to yourself, most of the even greatest sceptics can be convinced over time. And if not – be willing to accept it and respect your own choice

4. Only if there is fire in you, can you spark the fire in others: over time, your own passion can carry over to others and inspire them

5. Not only the final result counts. The journey is the destination

YOUR PATH TO POSITIVE IMPACT

Criteria for positive impact

'We soon forget what we have not deeply thought about.' ***Marcel Proust***

Before the inspiration from the previous chapters fades away, we invite you to reflect briefly on your reading experience, write down some thoughts and then read on for more details and suggestions.

Which story inspired me most?

- What was it about it? A specific issue, the specific skills or creativity of a person, the familiarity of environments or topics?

- What experiences or passions do you share with that person?

- Was there a specific aspect that touched something that has been on your mind for some time?

- In which story did you not find yourself, at all? What was wrong with it?

We live in a time in which more and more people are seeking sense and fulfilment in their profession and want their work to be meaningful for the community in which they live. Instead of functioning merely as a cog in the machine, they want to leave a positive mark on society and make a contribution towards a better world. The increasing intensity of regulations, processes and systems in many corporations and the striking clash of values between private and business lives make people want to escape. Maybe you are part of a growing number of seekers who are asking themselves whether their current occupation will permanently make them happy?

On the following pages we have assembled some inspirations that will hopefully support your development. We want to send you on your way with them. These inspirations are yet again the result of over 200 conversations that we have held: they reflect what people have experienced in life and show what we were able to learn during our many wonderful and special meetings. We hope that these inspirations provide enough food for thought and motivation for you to think about your current occupation from a different perspective. To change the direction of your professional life requires a lot of courage and a certain appetite for risk. But it is worth it. Luckily there is the insight that working towards a better, more sustainable and liveable world is a source of deep joy and satisfaction.

The concept of 'sustainable well-being' – a compass for your way to a happier life

It becomes clear to many people around the world that the systems we built in the last 200 years will not be the right ones for the next 200 years and beyond. These systems are not only supported by those who use them, but also by those who work for 'old-style' companies and service providers, that give them their energy and creativity. If we want to make a positive contribution to society with our profession, we have to reflect on the effects our job potentially has and start shaping them in the most positive way.

Based on this insight, we came across the concept of 'sustainable well-being' and believe that it is very useful when you are trying to assess the impact of your activities, especially the professional ones. We want to invite you to learn about it and to use it for your own professional development.

Your job and its effect

What do you know about your current occupation's effects? What and who is being influenced by it? Are you having a positive effect on other people's lives when you do your job successfully?

What are the criteria for whether or not your job has a positive or negative impact? Could it be an increase in salary, a powerful position, a bigger car or house? It was very clear to us that classical measures of success as they are commonly applied in our society will not answer this question.

The remaining question

We have tried to give an intuitive answer first and next we have constructed an explanation involving the idea of sustainability: an activity was positive if it led to something that was ecologically sensible, socially responsible and, at best, financially stable. However, we had a feeling that this was only good to begin with, but not yet sufficient for our purpose. Sustainability or sustainable development seemed to be a good means to an end, but it couldn't be the end per se.

Sustainable well-being as a measure

What is well-being?

From our interview research and company Forma Futura, we learned that in the *Millennium Ecosystem Assessment Report* over 1,300 leading biological scientists have developed an extensively researched and worldwide applicable model for what humans consider 'well-being'. It consists of the following five most important components and their 13 subcomponents. We believe that most people want all of this.

1. Material foundations for a good life
   - Adequate livelihoods
   - Sufficient nutritious food
   - Shelter
   - Access to goods

2. Health
   - Strength, i.e. physical well-being/strength
   - Feeling well, i.e. psychological well-being
   - Access to clean air and clean water

3. Security
   - Personal safety
   - Secure access to resources
   - Security from disasters

4. Good social relations
   - Social cohesion
   - Mutual respect
   - Ability to help others

5. Freedom of choice and action

If all these components are at least partially present, we can speak of a person's well-being, a distinct quality of life – regardless of residence, nationality or environment. Based on this model, we suggest that an activity that influences at least one or more of these components positively – and no others negatively, is possible as well as positive. Any activity that does not meet this requirement is seen as neutral in the best case – possibly even negative at worst. Below can be seen the components of well-being versus life under subliminal conditions, which are based on the model of the *Millennium Ecosystem Assessment Report*.

Poor welfare	Well-being
• Disenfranchisement	• Freedom of choice and action
• Vulnerability	• Security
• Bad health	• Good health
• Shortage of material foundations	• Material foundations of a good life
• Subliminal social relations	• Good social relations

What about your work? For instance, does your job have an impact on the health of others because you are working in pharmaceutical research? Who is affected by your work? Are you working on medical treatments that improve life a bit more for those who are already well-off? Or are you helping in the combat against serious diseases? To drive home the point: are you serving the development of Botox or of malaria medication? Or is your impact of an indirect nature? Perhaps because you work in education, you foster personal development and empower people to maintain their life?

Sustainability: Being aware of limited natural resources

Why is well-being not sufficient as a criterion? Why do we have to add the component of sustainability? Throughout centuries of human history this was not an imminent question because the number of people inhabiting the planet and their pursuit of well-being was not able to seriously threaten the natural foundations on which we live. But, with global population rising from one to seven billion in the last century alone and with estimates predicting at least another three-billion humans within the next 40 years, our situation has fundamentally changed. The depletion of resources has dramatically increased, and the foundation of life is massively threatened for many people.

Against this background, the idea of limitation and the concept of sustainability – and even sufficiency – gain more and more importance. We define systems as sustainable if they work in a way that does not destroy the natural foundations of life even if everyone makes use of them.

That is why we should always consider whether improvements to our own well-being would also be possible if more or even all human beings lived like us. The same holds for companies you support with your work and money: do they offer products and services that increase well-being according to the model we introduced above? Or do they produce positive results for a few at the cost of reducing the well-being of many?

Sustainable well-being for a happier life

In many human societies around the globe, maximising the material side of life has increasingly occupied the centre stage during the last decades. For many people, money has lost its function as a means to reach certain ends, and has turned into a purpose in and of itself. But are we happier because of that? We went on a global tour because despite our material success, we did not become happier. Our well-being did not increase along with the increase in success and income. Of course one can find distractions in new activities and hobbies, sumptuous parties or extravagant luxuries, but this has nothing to do with increasing well-being in the sense we have discussed above. We are now convinced that sustainable well-being can serve us as a very helpful tool in evaluating the outcome of potentially positive activities.

The following pages are an invitation for you to reconsider your professional activities against this background. Maybe it can help you evaluate your situation today. Perhaps you will find reason for reorientation and new development.

Five paths to a job with meaning

Preliminary thoughts

Whatever your professional occupation – reflect on the impact you have with it on the different components of well-being: basic needs, health, security, good social relations and freedom of choice and action. The following questions can support your assessment:

- What influence do I have on the well-being of others with my work? And precisely on which people?

- Where do I have indirect influences that I was not aware of?

- Who benefits from my work?

- Who could be harmed by it under certain circumstances?

- Can I change or reinterpret my occupation in a way that it leads to positive impact on others? And if so, how can I do it?

In order to reflect on your very personal attitude towards your job, you can ask yourself these questions:

- Will I be able to look back on my professional experience and results with satisfaction one day? What would I like to tell my grandchildren?

- Would I do this job even if I did not get paid for it or if my material needs were already satisfied?

- Would I continue doing what I am doing if I knew I was going to die soon?

Looking for the right job

Did any of these questions make you reflect deeply? Did they resonate with anything that has been on your mind for some time?

There are many ways to step into the unknown, many paths to follow. The path that suits you individually will pose a challenge, and it will not always be easy to manage. But it offers a chance to become happier and more satisfied.

In order to facilitate and support your journey we elaborated on five paths we came across during our world trip (see Figure 1). They reflect the experiences of our partners in conversation: those who we introduced in this book and those on our website. These men and women found their current occupation through one of these paths or a combination of them – some of them were more aware of it, others less so. However, the paths are alternative routes with a common end: finding an occupation with a positive impact.

Consider the questions we propose for each path in order to fully benefit from this model. It is not important to give a good answer to all the questions at once. It is much more important to consider them regularly, so that they take effect over time and lead you towards a job that fits you and has a positive impact on society. While the paths and questions are described in a very structured and rational way, a lot of decisions are made based on deep gut feeling. Do not forget to ask your stomach and heart for their opinion, let your intuition work and be honest with yourself.

Figure 1. **PATHS LEADING TO AN OCCUPATION WITH POSITIVE IMPACT**

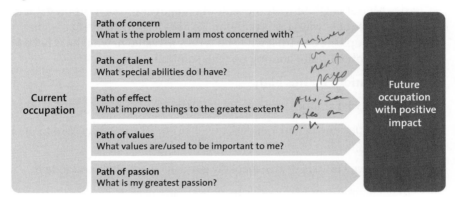

1. Path of concern
This path begins with a concern, a serious deficit that has been troubling your mind again and again. Many of our interview partners had identified a problem, a true concern that was missing a satisfying solution. Often they became aware of this problem through travelling, working or reading and could not proceed without solving it. With imperturbable belief they worked on a solution, until they were able to convince others to help them solve the issue. Karen Tse is the prototype of this path. As she helped rebuild the Cambodian judicial system, she had to experience on a daily basis what brutal consequences legal systems have for many innocent people if they are improperly implemented. She could not accept this situation and saw a solution: Karen founded the organisation International Bridges to Justice.

Principal questions for this path

- What are the problems in this world that I am most concerned with (for instance when I watch the news)? What bothers me in particular?
- Is there a concern I always wanted to match with a good solution – but I simply have never taken the time to do so?

- Have I already invested thoughts in the solution of a certain problem, perhaps even come up with some ideas for a solution?

Safia Minney and David Suzuki are two more examples of people who set off on this path.

2. Path of talent

The path of talent concentrates on your capacities, on you as a gifted individual who can use his or her talent in a positive way. Considerations like this caused several of our interview partners to occupy new positions in their organisations and enterprises, or even to create new positions. Again, others founded their own organisations in order to fully capitalise on their talent and potential.

Charles Maisel is gifted with the skill of recognising social problems and developing adequate ways to solve them. He likes leaving daily management issues up to people he can trust while he is fully invested in what he is best at: recognising problems and coming up with solutions.

Principal questions for this path

- What special abilities and talents do I have? *Building models in DB and Spreadsheets, Sailing. Forign Language + Good memory,*

- What experiences and networks do I bring to the table? What can I build on? *FSA, Microinsurance networking, St. bishko ume missionss, my exam students are a network.*

- What have I always been especially good at – back then and today? *Memorizing and passing tests.*

- In what areas would my skills be particularly useful? *Teaching,*

- Which solutions could benefit from my abilities? *Microinsurance orgs.*

The stories of Chris Eyre or Dr V are inspiring examples of this path.

3. Path of effect

At the starting-point of this path you consider different problems in your surroundings or on a more global scale. With a set of problems in mind, you concentrate your energy on finding the most effective way to improve the situation. Among our interviewees there were impressive people who took a very systematic approach to this search. They pondered diligently on what they consider to be the greatest problems and challenges on earth and what the most effective solutions to these problems are. Then they did what they could to move things in the right direction.

Thilo Bode tried out different approaches. Today he thinks that the greatest effect is reached when the interests of individual citizens are combined. In order to use this effect, he founded his own organisation, Foodwatch.

Principal questions for this path

- Where do I see the biggest challenges for humanity or my environment?

See p. 213

- What would be the most effective way of meeting these challenges? *reduce...*
Bring the poor to the line in USA, cd ship American to poor cntries. Reduce US national debt by shinks military,
- What are the most important switches that need to be operated, in order for this way to be successful?

- How can I help to bring these switches into the right position?

People who took this path are Amory Lovins and Maria Emilia Correa.

4. Path of values

Some people chose their profession because they were rooted in values and driven by strong ideals. However, these moved out of sight over time. Some of our interview partners returned to these values and ideas after many years of work. After they noticed that their current job had little to do with their original attitude, they changed their job environment.

Mariana Galarza is such an example: fascinated with the life stories of great doctors, she wanted to be a medical practitioner herself. But during her studies she recognised that the medical discipline was mostly concerned with sick people, and not with the conservation of health and well-being. Mariana turned this unbearable situation into something positive, by founding her own organisation and initiating a change of paradigms.

Principal questions for this path

- Which values and ideals were important to me when I chose my profession?
- What values am I missing in my current work? *Actuarial work is more about making profits than helping the old + poor*
- Are there areas or organisations that coincide with my ethical convictions? *World Vision.*

Florian Krämer and Ashok Khosla also chose the path of ideals.

5. Path of passion

In essence, this path is concerned with the passion that perhaps became your profession – or perhaps didn't, but should be part of your professional life. Finding a way of (re-)uniting passion and profession is the task of this path. A good example for this approach is Mia Hanak, who developed a passion for nature during long periods of travelling. Later she combined this with her studies of art history and museum science. The Natural World Museum is an innovative result that depicts the challenges of environmental protection in a very vivid and inspiring way.

Principal questions for this path

- What have I always been very passionate about? *Sailing. travel to developing countries Fuel Goes Sharp,*
- Did I perhaps have a professional option I did not choose, but that would have fitted in better with my passion? *economics. Pilot, boat captain,*
- How could I make a positive impact with my passion? *Write about mission trips to inspire others + lead mission trips*
- How could I combine my passion with my professional skills? *microinsurance for fishermen?*
- Can I integrate my passion into my job so that it makes sense? Or can I find other people or organisations I could get involved with professionally without leaving my passions behind? *St Luke world millions, See Forex p.v*

Other people with whom you can find inspiration for this path are Inés Sanguinetti and Vicky Colbert de Arboleda.

Finding your own path

As you have seen, many paths can lead to a job that has a positive impact. All our interviewees travelled these paths in their own individual way, often unconsciously. What would a new sense-driven path look like for you?

Also, at this stage you might want to exchange thoughts with people who share your concerns. Let yourself be inspired by the leading example of others. You can study the web pages of our partners and inform yourself about organisations and networks that are active in this field. Some suggestions for additional reading are attached in the reference list in back of this book.

An idea becomes reality – options to help you realise a job with positive impact

Clarify your options

While thinking through the questions you probably came across answers and options that could lead to a professional future. Bring them to life in front of your inner eye, and make this vision as concrete as possible. Describe each option in a few sentences. Why does it appeal to you?

Prioritise your preference

In order to distinguish your preference from the different options, question them with help of the following criteria:

Joy and passion
Which option would make me happiest in the long run? Which option could I develop the greatest passion for?

Talent and potential
Does this option fit my talent and potential? Be courageous as you answer this question. As the life stories of our partners in conversation show, there hardly is a thing that cannot be reached if you really want it.

Your way of life
Can I integrate this option with my way of life? Can I realise it within the vision I have of a good life? Does it go together with my other needs? These questions are more important than they seem at first. We came to know a number of people whose jobs allow them to have a positive impact on society, but they are still unhappy again and again. It turned out that they were very much absorbed by their profession, giving it a lot of attention and energy, while they were neglecting other parts of their life. We suggest that you take a closer look at the following seven areas of your life, and become aware of their importance:

1. Occupation and career

2. Family and private life

3. Income and savings

4. Health and fitness

5. Spirituality and inner peace

6. Personal growth and development

7. Involvement in community and society

Individually, having a sensible balance can mean different things. It could mean that you dedicate all your time to your job. It could also mean that this portion of your life should become a lot smaller because you need free time and time for your family. Besides work, you might also be very dedicated to your community.

Sustainable well-being
What is the ultimate contribution that an option makes to sustainable well-being? In order to answer this question, using the overview of components of sustainable well-being will prove to be helpful.

Check your preference

Important basic questions serve as a last test: Did you identify one or two options? Then return to the following questions and ask them again:

- Which values and ideals does this occupation correspond to? Are these indeed my own values?

- Would this occupation speak to my experience and full potential? What do I eventually have to learn in addition?

- Would I do this job if I did not get paid for it or if I had no financial needs?

- Could I perform well in this job within the time I want to spend with work?

- Could I earn as much money with this preferred job as I would like to earn?

- What could the biggest obstacles be as I try to implement this option? Is there a possible plan B?

- What will I do if my plan doesn't work?

- What do I want to look back on at the end of my life, if I choose this job?

Make sure you also consider options that do not sound like the ultimate solution or calling. Very often other steps and experiences are helpful or necessary.

Courageous implementation

Be courageous as you set out on the path you found to be the best option based on your reflections and convictions. What all of our interview partners have in common is that they had the courage to leave their current comfort zone in order to search for their own way and walk their own path. Even though there is not 100% security, it is of central importance that you start. The journey is more important than the goal. Sometimes going the long way round will help in getting to know the landscape and the goal better. Trust yourself, your steps and your choice, they tend to be more than coincidence.

A former consultant and manager of luxury hotels from Hong Kong, who is now heading an organisation for exotic resorts with ecologically and socially responsible management, told us: 'I sometimes have the feeling that I trained and learned all my life for the job I have today.'

None of the people we have portrayed in this book has regretted following their inner voice. The experience of doing the right thing and being able to look back on this path with joy and pride at the end of their lives outweighed all doubts and every setback. Many of them told us they would continue doing what they are doing even if they were only minimally paid or received no payment at all. And most of them assured us they would even continue doing their job if they knew their life would end soon. How many of us can say this about our professional lives? We sincerely hope that you make your next steps in this direction.

We wish you success, luck and joy on the way!

Social business entrepreneurs are the solution

Dr Muhammad Yunus
Nobel Peace Prize Winner

On television in Bangladesh, I watched with great sadness the horrors Hurricane Katrina unleashed on New Orleans and the Gulf Coast. I was so tempted to be there to participate in the post-disaster activities as we have so much experience with these kinds of catastrophes. But I knew my American friends did, too. Having studied at Vanderbilt and travelled extensively in the affected areas, names of places and faces of people were so familiar. A friend of mine from Ecuador even sent me a picture taken in Biloxi, Mississippi, 39 years previously to remind ourselves that we were there!

The post-Katrina recovery is time to tap the social entrepreneurial spirit of the Gulf Coast. Based on lessons from years of disastrous floods and cyclones in Bangladesh, I have witnessed the resilience of people and the power of communities if organised and tapped. We need to remove the obstacles and barriers to unleashing people's creativity and participation in the reconstruction and rebuilding of their homes, businesses and lives.

In starting a small business or building a house, having collateral and a clean credit report to get a bank loan is often an insurmountable barrier for many people around the world, whether in Karachi or New Orleans. But not in Bangladesh, thanks to Grameen Bank and a growing number of micro-finance organisations that provide collateral-free loans to the poorest for self-employment, small enterprises and housing. And, I am happy to report that a growing global movement of micro-finance organisations in more than 100 countries are following suit.

The United Nations declared 2005 the Year of Microcredit to focus attention on the scaling up of this solution. The Microcredit Summit Campaign, launched in 1997 at a time when we were reaching only 7 million people, is ready to announce that we have achieved or come very close to reaching 100 million of the world's poorest families, especially women, with credit for self-employment and other business services. But what does this mean for the Gulf Coast?

Credit for self-employment and small business enterprises, as well as housing finance, must be a part of the recovery package for the Gulf Coast. Savings and other financial services should be a part of these programmes just as they are in good micro-credit programmes and in Grameen Bank.

There are empowering ways to structure and deliver these programmes that respect the dignity and capacity of people. This is critical to preserve, protect and promote. The social capital of the Gulf Coast must be used to rebuild the communities in ways that strengthen them. We can never let them dissolve into violence and chaos again. Grameen works in self-organised groups of five, who then come together in centres of ten to 12 groups. They become the unit where the business is transacted. They also provide peer support and solidarity. This will be very important during the recovery period. People can help and learn from one another as they embark on the long road to normality.

Before Hurricane Katrina, people in New Orleans were already expressing an interest in social entrepreneurship. Not long ago, more than 500 people, including the mayor, came to hear a talk at Tulane University, New Orleans about Grameen Bank and other social entrepreneurial initiatives. Prior to Hurricane Katrina, people in New Orleans were organising in groups known as Prosperity Clubs and were exploring starting a Grameen-like programme. They had just opened a new branch of a credit union in Central City. They were planning to introduce entrepreneurship into the curriculum in high schools and encourage student ventures.

Even though the area lacked big business, the people knew that they had the strengths within them to foster opportunity where economic apartheid had created deep inequalities and resentment.

I know that Bangladeshis are good credit risks in spite of disasters such as floods, because they will always rebuild. They are deeply attached to their villages, their 'place'. I see the same love of one's community coming from the people in the Gulf Coast. This is a resource that must be tapped.

My most important piece of advice: create a social business initiative fund with a portion of the money being allocated for generating innovative ideas. Social businesses are businesses operated with social objectives, rather than money-making objectives. These are non-loss businesses to maximise benefits to the community without losing money. Encourage local people to come up with business ideas for rebuilding and improving their communities which will also create jobs. Back those social entrepreneurs – people who bring business discipline and metrics to creating positive social change. This will channel entrepreneurial talent, not for short-term financial profit and personal gain, but for solving social problems and accomplishing a public purpose.

These ideas can draw on business skills and use market forces. There is no shortage of money. But we need business ideas to make this money work for people. There are many creative ways to use all of the money that the public and government have pledged for the victims of this disaster. Some institutions for change should be given capital so that they may continue working for generations to come. Now is the time to unleash the spirit of social entrepreneurship.

Capitalism is interpreted too narrowly

Many of the problems in the world remain unresolved because we continue to interpret capitalism too narrowly. In this narrow interpretation we create a one-dimensional human being to play the role of entrepreneur. We insulate them from other dimensions of life, such as religious, emotional and political dimensions. They are dedicated to one mission in their business lives – to maximise profit. They are supported by masses of one-dimensional human beings who back them up with their investment money to achieve the same mission. The game of the free market works out beautifully with one-dimensional investors and entrepreneurs. We have remained so mesmerised by the success of the free market that we have never dared to express any doubt about it. We have worked extra hard to transform ourselves, as closely as possible, into the one-dimensional human beings as conceptualised in theory to allow the smooth functioning of the free market mechanism.

Economic theory postulates that you are contributing to the society and the world in the best possible manner if you just concentrate on squeezing out the maximum for yourself. When you get your maximum, everybody else will get their maximum.

As we devotedly follow this policy, sometimes doubts appear in our mind whether we are doing the right thing. Things don't look so good around us. We quickly brush off our doubts by saying all these bad things happen because of 'market failures'; well-functioning markets cannot produce unpleasant results.

I think that things are going wrong not because of market failure. It is much deeper than that. Let us be brave and admit that it is because of 'conceptualisation failure'. More specifically, it is the failure to capture the essence of a human being in our theory. Everyday human beings are not one-dimensional entities, they are excitingly multidimensional and indeed very colourful. Their emotions, beliefs, priorities and behaviour patterns can be more aptly described by drawing analogy with the basic colours and the millions of colours and shades they produce.

Social business entrepreneurs can play a big role in the market

Suppose we postulate a world with two kinds of people, both one-dimensional, but having different objectives. One type is the existing type, i.e. profit-maximising type. The second type is a new type, those who are not interested in profit-maximisation. They are totally committed to make a difference to the world. They are social-objective driven. They want to give a better chance in life to other people. They want to achieve their objective through creating/supporting sustainable business enterprises. Their businesses may or may not earn profit, but like any other business, they must not incur losses. They create a new class of business which we may describe as 'non-loss' business.

Can we find the second type of person in the real world? Yes, we can. Aren't we familiar with 'do-gooders'? Do-gooders are the same people who are referred to as 'social entrepreneurs' in formal parlance. Social entrepreneurism is an integral part of human history. Most people take pleasure in helping others. All religions encourage this quality in human beings. Governments reward them by giving tax breaks. Special legal facilities are created for them so that they can create legal entities to pursue their objectives.

Some social entrepreneurs (SEs) use money to achieve their objectives, some just give away their time, talent, skill or such other contributions which are useful to others. Those who use money may or may not try to recover part or all of the money they put into their work by charging a fee or price.

We may classify the SEs who use money into four types:

1. No cost recovery

2. Some cost recovery

3. Full cost recovery

4. More than full cost recovery

Once a SE operates at 100% or beyond the cost recovery point, they have entered the business world with limitless possibilities. This is a moment worth celebrating. They have overcome the gravitational force of financial dependence and are now ready for space flight! This is the critical moment of significant institutional transformation. They have moved from the world of philanthropy to the world of business. To distinguish them from the first two types of SEs listed above, we'll call them 'social business entrepreneurs' (SBEs).

With the introduction of SBEs, the marketplace becomes more interesting and competitive. Interesting because two different kinds of objectives are now at play creating two different sets of frameworks for price determination. Competitive because there are more players now than ever before. These new players can be equally aggressive and enterprising in achieving their goals as the other entrepreneurs.

SBEs can become very powerful players in the national and international economy. Today, if we add up the assets of all the SBEs of the world, they would not add up to be even an ultra-thin slice of the global economy. It is not because they basically lack growth potential, but because conceptually we neither recognised their existence, nor made any room for them in the market. They are considered freaks, and kept outside the mainstream economy. We do not pay attention to them, because our eyes are blinded by the theories taught in our schools.

If SBEs exist in the real world, it makes no sense why we should not make room for them in our conceptual framework. Once we recognise them with supportive institutions, policies and regulations, norms and rules will come into being to help them become mainstream.

The market is always considered to be an utterly incapable institution to address social problems. However, the market can be recognised as an institution which significantly contributes to creating social problems (environmental hazards, inequality, health, unemployment, ghettoes, crimes, etc.). Since the market has no capacity to solve social problems, this responsibility is handed over to the state. This arrangement was considered as the only solution until command economies were created where the state took over everything, abolishing the market.

But this did not last long. With command economies gone, we are back to the artificial division of work between the market and the state. In this arrangement, the market is turned into an exclusive playground of the personal gain seekers, overwhelmingly ignoring the common interest of communities and the world as a whole.

With the economy expanding at an unforeseen speed, personal wealth reaching unimaginable heights, technological innovations making this speed faster and faster, and globalisation threatening to wipe out the weak economies and the poor people from the economic map, it is time to consider the case of SBEs more seriously than we ever did before. Not only is it not necessary to leave the market solely to the personal-gain seekers, it is extremely harmful to mankind as a whole to do that. It is time to move away from the narrow interpretation of capitalism and broaden the concept of the market by giving full recognition to SBEs. Once this is done, SBEs can flood the market and make the market work for social goals as efficiently as it does for personal goals.

The social stock market

How do we encourage the creation of SBEs? What are the steps that we need to take to facilitate the SBEs to take up bigger and bigger chunks of market share?

First we must recognise the SBEs in our theory. Students must learn that businesses are of two kinds:

1. Business to make money

2. Business to do good to others

Young people must learn that they have a choice to make – which kind of entrepreneur they would like to be. If we broaden the interpretation of capitalism even more, they'll have a wider choice of mixing these two basic types of proportions just right for their own taste.

Second, we must make the SBEs and social business investors visible in the marketplace. As long as SBEs operate within the cultural environment of present stock markets they will remain restricted by the existing norms and lingo of trading. SBEs must develop their own norms, standards, measurements, evaluation criteria and terminology. This can be achieved only if we create a separate stock market for social business enterprises and investors. We can call it the 'social stock market'. Investors will come here to invest their money for the cause in which they believe, and in the company they think is doing the best in achieving a particular mission. There may be some companies listed in this social stock market which are excellent at achieving their mission, while at the same time making a very attractive profit on the side. Obviously these companies will attract both kinds of investors, social-goal oriented as well as personal-gain oriented.

Making a profit will not disqualify an enterprise to be a social business enterprise. The basic deciding factor for this will be whether the social goal remains to be an enterprise's overarching goal, and it is clearly reflected in its decision-making. There will be well-defined stringent entry and exit criteria for a company to qualify being listed in the social stock market, and to lose that status. Soon companies will emerge that will succeed in mixing both social goals and personal goals. There will be decision rules to decide up to what point they still qualify to enter the social stock market, and at what point they must leave it. Investors must remain convinced that companies listed in the social stock market are truly social business enterprises.

Along with the creation of the social stock market, we will need to create rating agencies, appropriate impact assessment tools and indices to understand which social business enterprise is doing more and/or better than others – so that social investors are correctly guided. This industry will need its *Social Wall Street Journal* and *Social Financial Times* to bring out all the exciting, as well as the terrible, news stories and analyses to keep social entrepreneurs and investors properly informed and forewarned.

Within business schools we can start producing social MBAs to meet the demand of the SBEs, as well as preparing young people to become SBEs themselves. I think young people will respond very enthusiastically to the challenge of making serious contributions to the world by becoming SBEs.

We will need to arrange financing for SBEs. New bank branches specialising in financing social business ventures will have to arise. New 'angels' will have to show up on the scene. Social venture capitalists will have to join hands with the SBEs.

How to make a start

One good way to get started with creating social business enterprises will be to launch a design competition for them. There can be local, regional and global competitions. Prizes for the successful designs will come in the shape of financing for the enterprises, or as partnerships for implementing the projects.

All submitted social business proposals can be published so that these can become the starting points for the designers in the next cycles, or ideas for someone who wants to start a social business enterprise.

The social stock market itself can be started by a SBE as a social business enterprise. One business school or several business schools could join hands to launch this as a project and start serious business transactions.

Let us not expect that a social business enterprise will come up, from its very birth, with all the answers to a social problem. Most likely, it will proceed in steps. Each step may lead to the next level of achievement. Grameen Bank is a good example in this regard. In creating Grameen bank I never had a blueprint to follow. I moved one step at a time, always thinking that each step would be my last. But it was not. That one step led me to another step, a step which looked so interesting that it was difficult to walk away from. I faced this situation at every turn.

I started my work by giving small amounts of money to a few poor people without any collateral. Then I realised how good people felt about it. I needed more money to expand the programme. To access bank money, I offered myself as a guarantor. To get support from another bank, I converted my project as the bank's project. Later, I turned it into a central bank project. Over time, I saw that the best strategy would be to create an independent bank to do the work that we do. So we did. We converted the project into a formal bank, borrowing money from the central bank to lend money to the borrowers. Since donors became interested in our work and wanted to support us, we borrowed and received grants from international donors. At one stage, we decided to become self-reliant. This led us to focus our efforts on generating money internally by collecting deposits. Now Grameen Bank has more money in deposits than it lends out to borrowers. It lends out half a billion dollars each year in loans averaging under $200 to 4.5 million borrowers, without collateral, and maintains a 99% repayment record.

We introduced many programmes in the bank – housing loans, student loans, pension funds, loans to purchase mobile phones to become village telephone people, and loans to beggars to become door-to-door salespeople. One came after another.

If we create the right environment, SBEs can take up significant market share and make the market an exciting place for fighting social battles in ever innovative and effective ways.

Let's get serious about social business entrepreneurs. They can brighten up this gloomy world.

IV
APPENDICES

APPENDIX 1
Acknowledgements

It is a great pleasure to finally thank the many companions we had during the three years of our book project. We never took their support and help for granted and we highly appreciate it. It seems impossible to thank all of them in person. But it is likewise impossible not to mention some of them explicitly. We want to primarily thank:

- Over 230 interview partners from around the world, who were generous and willing to share their time and knowledge with us. They provided the basis for this book by letting us partake in their rich experiences in life. We hope to be able to publish more of their stories in the future

- All our supporters who established contact with our fascinating interview partners, who encouraged us to continue our trip and welcomed us all around the world. We especially thank the Schwab Foundation for Social Entrepreneurship, Ashoka, Avina, the World Business Council for Sustainable Development and its local partner organisations, Echoing Green, the Skoll Foundation, the Aspen Institute, The Natural Edge Project, Japan for Sustainability, WISE, LEVAL and many others. Without your work of many years in identifying and supporting social entrepreneurs the world would be a much poorer place, and our work would have produced much poorer results

- The people and organisations at home which provided us with freedom, inspiration, time and professional support during our work and helped us spread the stories of our interviewees: BonVenture, Forma Futura, Ballhaus Wording, oekom Publishing, Foundation of Aachen, Austrian Institute for Sustainable Development and many more

- Thank you also to all the others who gave us their friendship and support, but cannot be mentioned by name here. It has been so much fun to work with you! That we met you and got to know you is an honour and has been incredibly enriching for us

- We would also like to thank David Hünlich and Jessica Plummer who worked on the translation of this book, which was originally published in German. John Stuart, Dean Bargh and Lynn Thorley from Greenleaf Publishing were a highly professional editorial team which made working with them a great pleasure – thank you so much

- Last, but not least, our families and friends who couldn't always understand our plans and projects, but were always at our side with sincere goodwill and active support. Your feedback on our ideas and texts was invaluable. The word goes that one can only dream and dance freely on solid ground – something you gave to us again and again

Joanna Hafenmayer Stefańska and Wolfgang Hafenmayer

APPENDIX 2
List of interviewees
(in chronological order)

Europe – February to March 2005

Johannes Czwalina, Founder and Executive Director, Czwalina Consulting, Basel, Switzerland.

Maria Serena Porcari, Executive Director, Fondazione Dynamo, Milan, Italy.

Francesco Pozzobon, Project Manager, Fondazione Dynamo, Milan, Italy.

Doris Pfister, Director, International Committee of the Red Cross, Geneva, Switzerland.

Barbara Brunner, Post AG, Bern, Switzerland.

Reto Casanova, Swiss Federal Agency for Construction and Logistics (BBL), Bern, Switzerland.

Joachim Schoss, Founder, MyHandicap.com, Zurich, Switzerland.

Barbara Sadowska, Founder and Director, Barka Foundation for Mutual Help, Pozna, Poland.

Tomasz Sadowski, Founder and Director, Barka Foundation for Mutual Help, Pozna, Poland.

Jacek Strzemieczny, Founder, Center for Citizenship (CCE), Warsaw, Poland.

Dr Ernst Ulrich von Weizsäcker, Dean of Bren School of Environmental Sciences and Management, University of California, Santa Barbara, USA (former member of German parliament, Berlin, Germany).

Thilo Bode, Founder and Executive Director, Foodwatch, Berlin, Germany.

Pierre Fornallaz, Founder, Fairplay-Foundation, Basel, Switzerland.

Prof. Dr Franz Josef Radermacher, Director, Research Institute for Applied Knowledge Processing (FAW); Co-Founder of the Global Marshall Plan Initiative, Ulm, Deutschland.

Alexander Barkawi, Managing Director, SAM Indexes, Zurich, Switzerland.

Karen Tse, Founder and Executive Director, International Bridges to Justice, Geneva, Switzerland.

Dr Erwin Stahl, Managing Director, BonVenture Management GmbH, Munich, Germany.

Lech Walesa, Founder and President, Lech Walesa Foundation, Former Polish State President and Noble Prize Winner, Danzig, Poland.

Niels Koldewijn, Founder and Executive Director, FairGround Sessions, Amsterdam, the Netherlands.

Africa – April to May 2005

Anthea Rossouw, Founder and Executive Director, Dreamcatcher, Cape Town, South Africa.

Kwesi Kwaa Prah, Director, Centre for Advanced Studies of African Society (CASAS), Cape Town, South Africa.

Florian Krämer, Executive Director Indawo Yentsikelelo, A Benedictory for Children, Nyanga at Cape Town, South Africa.

Charles Maisel, Founder and Executive Director, Men on the Side of the Road, Cape Town, South Africa.

Methvin Tanner, Director for Sustainable Development, Spier Holding, Lynedoch, South Africa.

Peter Boexkes, HIV/AIDS-Adviser, Former Training Centre for Teachers (mandated by the German Development Aid Service), Maseru, Lesotho.

Simon Winter, Regional Director, TechnoServe Afrika, Johannesburg, South Africa.

Isaac Shongwe, Director Company Development, Barloworld; Founder and Executive Director Letsema Holding and Letsema Foundation, Johannesburg, South Africa.

Vusi Sibanyoni, Volunteer, City Year, Johannesburg, South Africa.

Tumi Mabato, Volunteer, City Year, Johannesburg, South Africa

Cat Gifford, Volunteer, City Year, Johannesburg, South Africa.

Tsholo Mogotsi, Founder GuideStar International in Africa and Adviser of the Nelson Mandela Foundation, Johannesburg, South Africa.

Ramatoulaye Diallo, Executive Director, Endeavor, Johannesburg, South Africa.

Michelle Folsom, Executive Director, PATH South Africa, Johannesburg, South Africa.

Sera Thomson, Employee, Pioneers of Change, Johannesburg, South Africa.

Gisèle Yitamben, Founder and President, ASAFE (Association for Support and Support to Women Entrepreneurs), Douala, Cameroon.

Njogu Kahare, Employee, Green Belt Movement (Organisation of Nobel Prize Winners Wangari Maathai), Nairobi, Kenya.

Peter Wahome, Executive Director, People to People Tourism and Craftsmanship in Africa, Nairobi, Kenya.

Johnni Kjelsgaard, Founder, GrowthAfrica Advising, Nairobi, Kenya.

Adam Tuller, Executive Director, African Foundation of Nature Conservation, Nairobi, Kenya.

Nick Moon, Co-Founder and Director Africa, KickStart, Nairobi, Kenya.

South Asia – May to June 2005

Dr Ashok Khosla, Founder and President, Holding Development Alternatives, New Delhi, India.

Lisa Heydlauff, Founder and Executive Director, Going to School, New Delhi, India.

Gunter Pauli, President, Zero Emissions Research and Initiatives (ZERI), Tokyo, Japan.

Dr Henry Thiagaraj, Founder and Director, Foundation for the Freedom and Education of Dalits, Chennai, India.

Dr J. Jane Shanthakumari, Founder and Principal, LORD, Chennai, India.

Lalitha Rajaram, Manager, SIAAP, Chennai, India.

Paul Basil, Founder and Executive Director, Rural Innovation Network, Chennai, India.

M.P. Vasimalai, Founder and Director, DHAN Foundation, Madurai, India.

Dr Govindappa Venkataswamy† (Dr V), Founder and President, Aravind Eye Correction, Madurai, India.

Prof. Dr G. Natchiar, Director of the Eye Corrections Clinic, Aravind Eye Clinic, Madurai, India.

Dr Aravind Srinivasan, Manager and Eye Surgeon, Aravind Eye Clinic, Madurai, India.

Roma Debabrata, Founder and President, STOP (Stop Trafficking and Oppression of Children and Women), New Delhi, India.

Meera Bhattarai, Founder and Executive Director, Association of Craft Producers, Kathmandu, Nepal.

Bir Bahadur Ghale, President, Nepal Micro-Hydro Entrepreneurs' Federation, Kathmandu, Nepal.

Rajendra Mulmi, President, Youth Initiative, Kathmandu, Nepal.

Chetan Sharma, Founder and Director, Datamation and Datamation Foundation, New Delhi, India.

Anumita Roychowdhury, Executive Director (Research and Advocacy), Centre for Science and Environment (CSE), New Delhi, India.

Shantharam Shenai, Founder and Project Manager, Society of Green Crosses, Mumbai, India

Leila Karnik, Programme Manager, Wadhwani Foundation, Mumbai, India.

Shaheen Mistri, Founder and Executive Director, Akanksha Foundation, Mumbai, India.

Matthew Spacie, Founder and President, Magic Bus, Mumbai, India.

South-East and East Asia – July to September 2005

Conrado S. Heruela, Project Coordinator, Food and Agriculture Organization of the United Nations (FAO), Bangkok, Thailand.

Pairojana Sornjitti, Vice President, Population and Community Development Association (PDA), Bangkok, Thailand.

Dr Wolfgang Frank, Senior Adviser, Population and Community Development Association (PDA), Bangkok, Thailand.

Jessie L. Todoc, Senior Project Coordinator, CEERD (Centre for Energy Environment Resources Development), Bangkok, Thailand.

Daniel Siegfried, Co-Founder, Child's Dream, Chiang Mai, Thailand.

Marc Jenni, Co-Founder, Child's Dream, Chiang Mai, Thailand.

Maria Attard, Director of Operations Phnom Penh, HAGAR, Phnom Penh, Cambodia.

Jackie Keenan, Chief Operation Officer, HAGAR, Phnom Penh, Cambodia.

Paul Cleves, Founder and Director, Saigon Child Welfare, Ho Chi Minh City, Vietnam.

Dr Vo-Tong Xuan, Principal and Professor for Agriculture, University of Angiang, Long Xuyen City, Vietnam.

Jimmy Pham, Founder and Director, KOTO (Know One, Teach One), Hanoi, Vietnam.

Jaime Frias, National Director, International Development Enterprises (IDE), Hanoi, Vietnam.

Andrew Thomson, Executive Director, Economic and Environment, Hong Kong, China.

Wai On Leung, Executive Director, Waste and Environmental Technologies, Hong Kong, China.

Andrew Jones, Protector, Refugee Services, Hong Kong, China.

Martin Williams, Author, Photographer, Environmentalist, Hong Kong Outdoors, Hong Kong, China.

Charles Frew, Director, Asiatic Marine, Hong Kong, China.

Daniel Cheng, Executive Director, Dunwell Group; Dunwell Environmental-Tech (Holding), Hong Kong, China.

Stephen Fong, Executive Director, Swire Properties, Hong Kong, China.

Albert Oung, Founder and Executive Director, Roots Biopack, Hong Kong, China.

Raymond Lo, Executive Director, Samond Traders Holding, Hong Kong, China.

Cathy Zellweger, Director, International Cooperation, Caritas Hong Kong, Hong Kong, China.

Stanedy Yue, Environmental and Quality Manager, Philips Consumer Electronics, Hong Kong, China.

Ilse Massenbauer-Strafe, Founder, Oxyvital, Hong Kong, China.

Yongchen Wang, Environmental Journalist, Beijing, China.

Sarah Sable, Project Manager, PlaNet Finance, Beijing, China.

Lixin Fu, Professor and Director, Air Contamination Research, Tsinghua University, Beijing, China.

Hehe Zhang, Project Manager, Friends of Nature, Beijing, China.

Lisa Wu, Student, Founder and President, SIFE (Students In Free Enterprise) Beijing, Beijing University for Foreign Languages, Beijing, China.

Bonnie Wang, Student and Volunteer, Journalism and Communication Department, Beijing Sports University, Beijing, China.

Dolores van Dongen, Founder and Executive Director, Sunshine Learning Centre, Beijing, China.

Qing Wu, Professor, Beijing University for Foreign Languages, Beijing, China.

Christoph Moellers, President, Holcim Beijing, Beijing, China.

Andrew Lee, Assistant Director, Cheung Kong Centre for Proceedings and Conflict Elimination, Beijing, China.

Markus tho Pesch, Director Beijing Office, DEG – German Investment and Developmental Agency, Beijing, China.

Claudia Wink, Investment Manager for Special Programmes, DEG – German Investment and Development Agency, Beijing, China.

Glenn Frommer, Sustainability Manager, Mass Transit Railway (MTR), Hong Kong, China.

Renée Berman, Investments for Discriminated Populations, Credit Suisse First Boston (Hong Kong), Hong Kong, China.

Annie Wu, Standing Committee Member, The National Committee of Chinese People's Political Consultative Conference; Vice Chairman, Beijing Air Catering Co.; Board Member, World Trade Center Association, Hong Kong, China.

Graham Lane, Executive Director, Asiatic Environmental Group of Bovis Lend Lease, Tokyo, Japan.

Dr Kiyohiko G. Nishimura, Member of the Highest-Ranking Political Council, Bank of Japan, Tokyo, Japan.

Junko Edahiro, Executive Director, Japan for Sustainability Tokyo, Japan.

Yusuke Saraya, President, Saraya Co., Osaka, Japan.

Hitoshi Suzuki, Head Manager Social Contributions Department, Communication for Corporate Social Responsibility, NEC, Tokyo, Japan.

Safia Minney, Founder and President, People Tree, Fair Trade Company, Tokyo, Japan.

Lena Lindahl, Japan Representative, Swedish Sustainability Association, Tokyo, Japan.

Yutaka Okayama, Manager, Planning Group Environmental Affairs, Toyota, Tokyo, Japan.

Yoshiyuku Tsuji, Group Manager, Environmental Association, Tokyo Electric Power Company (TEPCO), Tokyo, Japan.

Maeda Shigenori, Employee, Environmental Administration, Tokyo Electric Power Company (TEPCO), Tokyo, Japan.

Takafumi Masaki, Employee, Environmental Administration, Tokyo Electric Power Company (TEPCO), Tokyo, Japan.

Joel Challender, Coordinator of Translators, Peace Boat, Tokyo, Japan.

Yoshioka Tatsuya, Director, Peace Boat, Tokyo, Japan.

Hideyuki Inoue, Executive Director, ETIC. Social Venture Center, Tokyo, Japan.

Hiroyasu Ichikawa, Personal Consultant, AXIOM, Tokyo, Japan.

Takako Okamura, Organic Concierge, Tokyo, Japan.

Australia – October to November 2005

David Bussau, Founder, Maranatha Trust and Opportunity International, Sydney, Australia.

Benjamin Roche, Manager, Project Sustainable Living, University of New South Wales, Sydney, Australia.

Martin Green, Director, Photovoltaics Special Research Center, University of New South Wales, Sydney, Australia.

Chris Sorrell, Professor, School of Materials Science and Engineering, University of New South Wales, Sydney, Australia.

Nick Ashbolt, Professor and Head School of Civil and Environmental Engineering, University of New South Wales, Sydney, Australia.

Richard Jefferson, Executive Director, CAMBIA, Canberra, Australia.

Prashanth Shanmugan, Student, University of New South Wales, Volunteer and Speaker at ICRC, Sydney, Australia.

Janis Birkeland, Ecological Innovations at ESD, Canberra, Australia.

Michael Smith, Scope Coordinator, The Natural Edge Project.

Dr Clive Hamilton, Director, The Australian Institute, Canberra, Australia.

Dexter Dunphy, Emeritus Professor of the School of Management, University of Technology, Sydney, Australia.

Nic Frances, Executive Director, EasyBeingGreen, Melbourne, Australia.

Alan Pears, Director, Exceptional Professor at RMIT University, Sustainable Solutions, Melbourne, Australia.

Victoria Wilding, Executive Director, Shift Foundation, Melbourne, Australia.

Caroline Bayliss, Co-Director, Global Sustainability Institute, Melbourne, Australia.

Charlie Hargroves, Project Coordinator, The Natural Edge Project, Adelaide, Australia.

Nick Palousis, Enterprise Coordinator, The Natural Edge Project, Adelaide, Australia.

Dan Atkins, Director, Sustainable Economic Practices, Adelaide, Australia.

John Brisbin, Coordinator, Environmental Centre, Alice Springs, Australia.

Lania Lynch, Environmental Management Coordinator, James Cook University, Cairns, Australia.

Peter Jackson, Partner, Jackson Smith Council, Sydney, Australia.

Dr Mark Diesendorf, Institute for Environmental Studies, University of New South Wales and Director of the Sustainability Centre, Sydney, Australia.

Ramsay Moodie, Director Corporate Affairs, Fuji Xerox Australia, Sydney, Australia.

May Miller-Dawkins, Programme Coordinator, Oxfam International Youth Parliament, Oxfam, Sydney, Australia.

Paul Gilding, Founding Partner, Ecos Corporation, Sydney, Australia.

North America – December 2005 to January 2006

Rick Aubry, PhD, President and Executive Director, Rubicon Program, Richmond, USA.

Jim Fournier, Founder, Planet Work and Eprida, San Francisco, USA.

James Fruchterman, President and Executive Director, Benetech, Palo Alto, USA.

Mia Hanak, Founder and Executive Director, Natural World Museum, San Francisco, USA.

Perla Ni, Editor in Chief, Stanford Social Innovation Review, San Francisco, USA. Current: Founder and Executive Director, VoterWatch.

Victor d'Allant, Executive Director, Social Edge, Skoll Foundation, Palo Alto, USA.

Timothy Freundlich, Director of Strategic Development, Calvert Foundation, San Francisco, USA.

Kevin Starr, Director, Mulago Foundation and Rainer Fellows, San Francisco, USA.

Chris A. Eyre, Executive Director, Legacy Venture, Palo Alto, USA.

Amanda Reilly, Responsible for Technological Distinctions, The Tech Museum of Innovation, San Jose, USA.

William Rosenzweig, Executive Director, Great Spirit Ventures, Mill Valley, USA.

Erin Keown Ganju, Executive Director (COO), Room to Read, San Francisco, USA.

Aron Hurst, President and Founder, Taproot Foundation, San Francisco, USA.

Heidi Krauel, Investment Manager, Pacific Community Ventures, San Francisco, USA.

Liz Maw, Executive Director, Net Impact, San Francisco, USA.

Jessica Jackley Flannery, Co-Founder, KIVA, Peer-to-Peer Darlehen, San Francisco, USA.

Matthew Flannery, Co-Founder, KIVA, Peer-to-Peer Darlehen, San Francisco, USA.

Philipp Kauffmann, Economic and Biodiversity-Equator Initiative, UNDP, New York, USA.

Peter Reiling, Vice President of Leadership and the Political Program, Aspen Institute, Washington, DC, USA.

Bruce McNamer, President and Executive Director, TechnoServe, Washington, DC, USA.

Stefanie Jowers, Former Director of Strategic Affairs and the Membership Department, National Peace Corps Association, Washington, DC, USA.

Michael Margolis, Founder, Thirsty-Fish, Washington, DC, USA.

Kelly Rusk, Founder, IYOKO, Director of Operating Systems and International Affairs, Wein America, Washington, DC, USA.

Justin Conway, Manager, Investment Program for Discriminated Communities, Co-op America and Social Investment Forum, Washington, DC, USA.

Björn-Sören Gigler, Information Director, Developmental Information, World Bank, Washington, DC, USA.

Ben Quinto, Executive Director, Global Teen Network (GYAN), New York, USA.

Abi Falik, Former Program Manager Global Citizen Corps, NetAid, New York, USA.

Keith Hammonds, Vice President, Editor in Chief *FastCompany Magazine*, New York, USA.

Jordan Kassalow, Founder and Executive Director, Scojo Vision and Scojo Foundation, New York, USA.

Sanda Balaban, Project Manager, Developmental Department New York, New York, USA.

Gina Rodolico, Director for Information and Communication, E+Co, New York, USA.

Caroline Kim Oh, Executive Director, iMentor, New York, USA.

Matthew Klein, Executive Director, Blue Ridge Foundation, New York, USA.

Reah-Janise Kauffman, Vice President, Earth Policy Institute, Washington DC, USA.

Amory Lovins, Founder and Executive Director, Rocky Mountains Institute, Snowmass, USA.

Amy Margerum, Finance Direktor and Direktor for Administration, Aspen Institute, Aspen, USA.

Hunter Lovins, Founder, Natural Capitalism, Boulder, USA.

Paul Polak, Founder and President, International Development Enterprises, Boulder, USA.

Guy Dauncey, Speaker, Author and Sustainability Adviser, World Future, Victoria, Canada.

Roger Colwill, Vice President Business Development, International Composting Corporation, Victoria, Canada.

Diana Lindley, Founder, Unity Flag Society, Victoria, Canada.

Mary-Wynne Ashford, Co-President, International Doctors for the Prevention of Nuclear War, Victoria, Canada.

David Suzuki, Author and President, David Suzuki Foundation, Vancouver, Canada.

Nola Kate Seymoar, President and Executive Director, International Center for Sustainable Cities (ICSC), Vancouver, Canada.

David Van Seters, President and Executive Director, Rural Supply of Small Potatoes (SPUD), Vancouver, Canada.

South America – January to March 2006

Isabel Viscarra, Bolivian Representative, Ashoka, La Paz, Bolivia.

Brigitte Brodmann, Volunteer, Psychological Support for Prisoners/Hostages, La Paz, Bolivia.

Sara Diestro, Founder and Executive Director, School of Sports and Life, Lima, Peru.

Albina Ruiz Ríos, Executive Director, Healthy City, Lima, Peru.

Hernando de Soto, Founder, President and Executive Director, Institute for Freedom and Democracy (ILD), Lima, Peru.

Baltazar Caravedo, Peru Representative, Avina, Lima, Peru.

Vicky Colbert de Arboleda, Founder and Executive Director, Escuela Nueva, Bogotá, Columbia.

Enrique Penalosa, Former Mayor of Bogotá, Founder and President, Foundation for the Country, that We Love, Bogotá, Columbia.

Catalina Cock Duque, Founder and Manager, Green Gold and Amichocó, Medellin, Columbia.

Bruce Mac Master, Chairman of the Advisory Board, Sharing with Columbian, Bogotá, Columbia.

Alejandro Martinez, Founder and Executive Director, Foundation Small Worker, Bogotá, Columbia.

Angelica Castro Rodriguez, Executive Director, TransMilenio, Bogotá, Columbia.

Dr Roberto Gutiérrez, Assistant Professor, Director of the Initiative Social Enterprise, University of Anden, Bogotá, Columbia.

Adriana Milanesi-Agnoli, Ecuador Representative, Ashoka, Quito, Ecuador.

Patricio Donoso, Adviser for Sustainable Development, Quito, Ecuador.

José Caraval, Gründer, Sustainable Rural Development, Quito, Ecuador.

Maria Elena Ordoñez, Founder and Executive Director, Arcandina, Quito, Ecuador.

Maria del Carmen Tene, Manager, Rights for Indigenous People, World Bank, Quito, Ecuador.

Mariana Galarza, Executive Director, Association Life, Quito, Ecuador.

Yolanda Kakabadse, Executive Director and President, Foundation Future Latin America, Quito, Ecuador.

Sonja Andrade, President, Merger for Social Organisations in Atenci, Quito, Ecuador.

Carlos Zapata, President, Foundation Galápagos, Puerto Ayora, Galapagos, Ecuador.

Maria Emilia Correa, Vice President for Social and Ecological Responsibility, Grupo Nueva, Santiago, Chile.

Marcela Zubieta Acuña, Executive Director and Vice President, Foundation: Our Children, Santiago, Chile.

Amalia Fischer, Main Coordinator, Fundo Angela Borba, Rio de Janeiro, Brazil.

André Porto, Co-Founder, Religion und Peace, VIVA! Rio, Rio de Janeiro, Brazil.

André Villas Boas, Manager, Socio-ecological Organisation, São Paulo, Brazil.

Pedro Tarak, Representative and Director Interregional Connections, Avina, Buenos Aires, Argentina.

Angelique Xanthopoulos, Founder and Director, Insight Argentina, Buenos Aires, Argentina.

Daniel Dickens, Coordinator, HelpArgentina, Buenos Aires, Argentina.

Rosalia Gutierrez, Founder and Director, Organisation of Native Students, CEPLA, Buenos Aires, Argentina.

Ricardo E. Bertolino, Founder and President of the Council, ecoclubes, Buenos Aires, Argentina.

Moira Rubio Brennan, Director, Foundation ph15, Buenos Aires, Argentina.

Inés Sanguinetti, Director, Foundation Crear Vale La Pena, Buenos Aires, Argentina.

Matías Laurenz, Co-Director, Action without Borders, Idealistas.org, Buenos Aires, Argentina.

Ami Dar, Executive Director, Idealist.org, Buenos Aires, Argentina.

Martin Churba, Designer and Executive Director, Tramando, Buenos Aires, Argentina.

Toty Flores, Member, The Movement of the Unemployed People of La Matanza, Buenos Aires, Argentina.

Teresa Urban, Journalist, Author and Independent Adviser, Curitiba, Paraná, Brazil.

Juara Ferreira, Director CBR Institute and Director Opet School, Opet School, Curitiba, Paraná, Brazil.

Jaime Lerner, Founder and President, Institute Jaime Lerner, Curitiba, Paraná, Brazil.

Silvia Ziller, Founder and Executive Director Hórus Institute and Director The Nature Conservancy, Curitiba, Paraná, Brazil.

Europe – April to May 2006

Doug Miller, President, European Venture Philanthropy Association, London, England.

Jost Hamschmidt, President, oikos Foundation for the Economy and, St Gallen, Switzerland.

Rolf Wüstenhagen, Co-Director, Institute for the Economy and the Environment (IWÖ-HSG), University St Gallen (HSG), St Gallen, Switzerland.

Mirjam Schöning, Director, Schwab Foundation for Social Entrepreneurship, Geneva, Switzerland.

Pamela Hartigan, Executive Director, Schwab Foundation for Social Entrepreneurship, Geneva, Switzerland.

Bernard Lietear, Professor, Institute for Sustainable Resource Management and Agriculture, University of California, Berkeley, USA.

APPENDIX 3
URL directory and literature

URL directory

- www.ashoka.org and www.changemakers.net
  Information about more than 2,000 social entrepreneurs worldwide and their innovations and societal solutions.

- www.aspeninstitute.org
  Politic think-tank executives worldwide who identify with and try to find solutions to social problems in their corresponding countries.

- www.avina.net/eng
  Information about organisations and people in Latin America that help solve social and ecological problems.

- www.bonventure.de/en/home.html
  First Venture Capital Company in German-speaking countries that invests in companies whose purposes relate to ecological and/or social issues. With that they try to maximise not the financial, but the social impact.

- www.echoinggreen.org
  An organisation that mainly supports very new initiatives and tries to implement innovative solutions in social and/or ecological realms.

- www.evpa.eu.com
  Association of the most important European organisations, especially those in venture philanthropy.

- www.guidestar.org
  A platform that provides information about non-profit organisations.

- www.globalgiving.com
  A platform that is informative concerning what can be accomplished with financial investments in certain projects and deals with making donations online.

- www.idealist.org
  An organisation that brings together people, ideas and organisations, and pushes the world towards positive change.

- www.myimpact.net
  An organisation that inspires and furthers people and solutions which in turn have a positive impact towards sustainable life quality.

- www.schwabfound.org
  An array of the world's best social entrepreneurs and their strategies, models and motivations for a better world.

- www.skollfoundation.org and www.socialedge.org
  Information about current issues and organisations in terms of social entrepreneurship.

- www.ssireview.org
  A magazine about social innovations.

- www.wbcsd.org
  WBCSD is an international organisation of companies that further sustainable development. The website includes publications and background information.

- www.wiserearth.org
  A platform that includes information about people and organisations that want to solve social and ecological problems in our world.

- www.nextbillion.net
  Resource platform for interesting information about the social investment sector.

Literature

Reading material concerning the topic 'How do I find a path in life?'

- Bridges, W. (2004) *Transitions: Making Sense of Life's Changes* (Cambridge, MA, USA: Da Capo Lifelong Books).
  Gives explanations and support on how to overcome difficult phases during life's changes.

- Bronson, P. (2003) *What Should I Do with My Life?* (New York: Random House, Inc.).
  An inspiring short story from people who found their own distinct careers.

- Canfield, J. (2005) *The Success Principles: How to Get from Where You Are to Where You Want to Be* (London: Element).
  A book that gives practical advice concerning making one's life more effective and more efficient.

- Covey, S.R. (2004) *The 7 Habits of Highly Effective People* (London: Simon & Schuster).
  The classic about principles for personal and occupational success (also visit: www.franklincovey.de).

- Covey, S.R. (2005) *The 8th Habit: From Effectiveness to Greatness* (New York: Free Press).
  Building on the deep understanding of The 7 Ways to Effectiveness, *the book helps to find one's inner voice.*

- Hawken, P. (2007) *Blessed Unrest* (New York: Penguin Books).
  Describes and explains why in the past years people created a worldwide movement with the purpose of dealing with ecological and social problems.

- Nash, L. and H. Stevenson (2004) *Just Enough* (New Jersey, USA: John Wiley & Sons, Inc.).
  Conception of successful people that defines their success not only in terms of financial success, but also how they are satisfied with all areas of their lives.

- O'Toole, J. (2005) *Creating the Good Life: Applying Aristotle's Wisdom to Find Meaning and Happiness* (Holtzbrinck Publishers: Ashford, Connecticut, USA).
  Provides good suggestions about how to become more effective in life, uses and translates Aristotle's wisdom into our modern world.

- Ray, P. and R. Anderson (2000) *The Cultural Creatives: How 50 Million People are Changing the World* (New York: Three Rivers Press).
  Description of a new type of person who wants to positively change the world.

- Tracy, B. (2012) *The Power of Self-confidence: Become Unstoppable, Irresistible, and Unafraid in Every Area of Your Life* (New Jersey, USA: John Wiley & Sons, Inc.).

- Tracy, B. (2007) *Eat that Frog!: 21 Great Ways to Stop Procrastinating and Get More Done in Less Time* (San Francisco, CA, USA: Berrett-Koehler Publishers, Inc.).
  Ways to accomplish the right things in less time.

- Tracy, B. (1995) *Maximum Achievement: Strategies and Skills that Will Unlock Your Hidden Powers to Succeed* (New York: Fireside, Simon & Schuster Inc.).
  Explains in a very structured manner how one can use concentrating on the most essential can lead to more success, freedom and income.

Reading material about social entrepreneurship, impact investing and philanthropy

- Ashton, R. (2010) *How to Be a Social Entrepreneur: Make Money and Change the World* (Chichester, UK: Capstone Publishing Ltd).
- Banerjee, A. and E. Duflo (2012) *Poor Economics: A Radical Rethinking of the Way to Fight Global Poverty* (USA: PublicAffairs, Perseus Books Group).
- Bloom, P.N. (2012) *Scaling Your Social Venture: Becoming an Impact Entrepreneur* (New York: Palgrave Macmillan).
- Bornstein, D. (2007) *How to Change the World: Social Entrepreneurs and the Power of New Ideas* (New York: Oxford University Press; updated edn).
  Stories about social entrepreneurs that changed the world through their organisations.
- Bornstein, D., and Davis, S. (2010) *Social Entrepreneurship: What Everyone Needs to Know* (New York: Oxford University Press Inc.).
- Brest, P., and H. Harvey (2008), *Money Well Spent: A Strategic Plan for Smart Philanthropy* (New York: Bloomberg Press).

- Bugg-Levine, A. and J. Emerson (2011) *Impact Investing: Transforming How We Make Money While Making a Difference* (San Francisco, CA, USA: Jossey-Bass).
- Collier, P. (2008) *The Bottom Billion: Why the Poorest Countries are Failing and What Can Be Done About It* (New York: Oxford University Press).
- Easterly, W.R. (2007) *The White Man's Burden: Why the West's Efforts to Aid the Rest Have Done So Much Ill and So Little Good* (New York: Penguin Books).
- Elkington, J., P. Hartigan and K. Schwab (2008) *The Power of Unreasonable People: How Social Entrepreneurs Create Markets that Change the World* (Boston, MA, USA: Harvard Business Press/Center for Public Leadership).
- Gary, T., K. Klein, S. Orman and N. Adess (2007) *Inspired Philanthropy: Your Step-by-Step Guide to Creating a Giving Plan and Leaving a Legacy* (San Francisco, CA, USA: Jossey-Bass).
- Lynch, K., and J. Walls, (2009) *Mission, Inc.: The Practitioners Guide to Social Enterprise* (San Francisco, CA, USA: Berrett-Koehler Publishers, Inc.).
- Nicholls, A. (2008) *Social Entrepreneurship: New Models of Sustainable Social Change* (New York: Oxford University Press).
- Nicholls, A. (2006) *Social Entrepreneurship: New Models of Sustainable Social Change* (New York: Oxford University Press).
  Theoretical fundamentals that concern social entrepreneurship.
- Praszkier, R., and A. Nowak (2011), *Social Entrepreneurship: Theory and Practice* (New York: Cambridge University Press).
- Saltman, K.J. (2010) *The Gift of Education: Public Education and Venture Philanthropy* (Education, Politics, and Public Life) (New York: Palgrave Macmillan).
- Schwartz, B., and Drayton (2012) *Rippling: How Social Entrepreneurs Spread Innovation throughout the World* (San Francisco, CA, USA: Jossey-Bass).
- Scofield, R. (2011) *The Social Entrepreneur's Handbook: How to Start, Build, and Run a Business that Improves the World* (New York: McGraw-Hill).
- Tierney, T.J., and J.L. Fleishman (2011) *Give Smart: Philanthropy that Gets Results* (New York: PublicAffairs, Perseus Books Group).
- Yunus, M. (2010) *Building Social Business: The New Kind of Capitalism that Serves Humanity's Most Pressing Needs* (New York: PublicAffairs, Perseus Books Group).

Reading material about values

- Ben-Shahar, T. (2007) *Happier: Learn the Secrets to Daily Joy and Lasting Fulfillment* (New York: McGraw-Hill).
- Bosshart, D. (2011) *The Age of Less* (Germany: Murmann Verlag).
- Jackson, T. (2011) *Prosperity without Growth: Economics for a Finite Planet* (London/New York: Earthscan).
- Ben-Shahar, T. (2010) *Being Happy: You Don't Have to Be Perfect to Lead a Richer, Happier Life* (USA: McGraw-Hill).
- Jansen Kraemer, H.M. (2011) *From Values to Action: The Four Principles of Values-Based Leadership* (San Francisco, CA, USA: Jossey-Bass).
- Lawrence J.T., and P.W. Beamish (2012) *Globally Responsible Leadership: Managing According to the UN Global Compact* (The Ivey Casebook Series) (California, CA, USA: Sage Publications, Inc.).

- Pless, N.M., and T. Maak (2012) *Responsible Leadership* (London/New York: Routledge).
- Wallis, J. (2011) *Rediscovering Values: A Guide for Economic and Moral Recovery* (New York: Howard Books).

Reading material about corporate social responsibility and companies' long-term responsibility

- Benioff, M., and K. Southwick (2004) *Compassionate Capitalism* (New Jersey, USA: Career Press).
  Theoretical reflections and examples of how companies can incorporate their businesses into making the world a better place.
- Benioff, M., and C. Adler (2007) *The Business of Changing the World: Twenty Great Leaders on Strategic Corporate Philanthropy* (New York: McGraw-Hill).
  Examples about how internationally operating companies can be just and fair with their social and ecological responsibilities.
- Esty, D.C., and A.S. Winston, (2007) *Green to Gold: How Smart Companies Use Environmental Strategy to Innovate, Create Value, and Build Competitive Advantage* (New Jersey, USA: John Wiley & Sons, Inc.).
  Strategies concerning companies can profit from ecological changes.
- Hamel, G. (2012) *What Matters Now: How to Win in a World of Relentless Change, Ferocious Competition, and Unstoppable Innovation* (San Francisco, CA, USA: Jossey-Bass).
- Kotler, P., and N. Lee (2004) *Corporate Social Responsibility: Doing the Most Good for Your Company and Your Cause* (New Jersey, USA: John Wiley & Sons, Inc.).
  Emphasises in a structured manner what corporate social responsibility can mean for companies and gives illustrative examples.
- Laszlo, C. (2003) *The Sustainability Company: How to Create Lasting Value through Social and Environmental Performance* (Washington, DC, USA: Island Press).
  Shows how companies can achieve long-term worth, while concerning themselves with the social and ecological components in their society.
- Lovins, L.H., M. Odum and J. W. Rowe (2011) *Reinventing Fire: Bold Business Solutions for the New Energy Era* (Colorado, USA: Rocky Mountain Institute).
- Lovins, L.H., and B. Willard (2005) *The Next Sustainability Wave: Building Boardroom Buy-in* (New Society Publishers: Gabriola Island, Canada).
  How one finds ideas of sustainability in big companies and how to win the support of policy makers.
- Ng, T. (2012) *Business Ethics and Sustainability* (Germany: Obiter Dicta).
- Prahalad, C.K. (2006) *The Fortune at the Bottom of the Pyramid* (New Jersey, USA: Pearson Education, Inc.).
  Account of how to integrate 4 million people who earn less than $2 per day into a market economy that obliterates poverty on earth, but simultaneously allows many companies to profit.

- Schmidheiny, S. (1993) *Changing Course: A Global Business Perspective on Development and the Environment* (Munich, Germany: MIT Press).
  Describes why companies and executives are responsible for sustainable development and what this could look like for these companies.

Reading material about sustainability

- Brown, L.R. (2012) *Full Planet, Empty Plates: The New Geopolitics of Food Scarcity* (New York: The Earth Policy Institute).
- Brown, L.R. (2011) *World on the Edge: How to Prevent Environmental and Economic Collapse* (New York: The Earth Policy Institute).
- Brown, L.R. (2009) *Plan B 4.0: Mobilizing to Save Civilization* (New York: The Earth Policy Institute).
  A realistic vision on how we can save our stressed planet and build a foundation for human civilisation.
- Carson, R. (2007) *Silent Spring* (New York: Houghton Mifflin Harcourt).
- De Soto, H. (2002) *The Mystery of Capital: Why Capitalism Triumphs in the West and Fails Everywhere Else* (New York: Basic Books).
  Analysis of why poverty cannot be eliminated with financial support alone.
- Hargroves, C., and M. Smith (2005) *The Natural Advantage of Nations* (London: Taylor & Francis, Inc.).
  Collection of theoretical concepts of sustainability.
- Lietaer, B. (2001) *Future of Money: Creating New Wealth, Work and a Wiser World* (London: Random House)
  Describes why our current monetary system will destroy our civilisation and how a monetary system should look in order to prevent this destruction.
- Lietaer, B., and S. Belgin (2011) *New Money for a New World* (USA: Qiterra Press).
- Lovins, A., L.H. Lovins and P. Hawken (2008) *Natural Capitalism* (New York: Back Bay Books).
  Shows how the next industrial revolution would have to be structured so that all of humanity could continue to live in a peaceful, just and thriving world.
- McDonough, W., and M. Braungart (2002) *Cradle to Cradle: Remaking the Way We Make Things* (New York: North Point Press).
  Looks at design in general, but especially what products and services should look like when creating systems that are capable of surviving and are forward-looking.
- Meadows, D.H., J. Randers and D.L. Meadows (2006) *Limits to Growth: The 30-Year Update* (London/New York: Earthscan).
- Pauli, G.A. (2010) *The Blue Economy: 10 Years, 100 Innovations, 100 Million Jobs* (New Mexico: Paradigm Publications).
- Porritt, J. (2007) *Capitalism: As if the World Matters* (London/New York: Earthscan).
  Shows from a very deep understanding of sustainability how boundaries that would conserve natural resources in a capitalistic society could look.

- Wackernagel, M., and W. Rees (1997) *Our Ecological Footprint: Reducing Human Impact on the Earth* (Gabriola Island, Canada: New Society Publishers). *Introduces the concept of an ecological footprint and shows that through this concept, the limitations on natural resources are understandable.*

Publications that include other interesting suggestions

- Habisch, A. (2003) *Corporate Citizenship* (Germany: Springer).
- Hart, S. (2005) *Capitalism at the Crossroads* (New Jersey: Pearson Education, Inc.).
- Kasser, T. (2002) *The High Price of Materialism* (Cambridge, MA, USA/London: MIT Press).
- Needleman, J. (1991) *Money and the Meaning of Life* (New York: Doubleday).
- Pearsall, P. (2005) *The Last Self-Help Book You'll ever Need* (New York: Perseus Books Group).
- Willard, B. (2002) *The Sustainability Advantage* (Gabriola Island, Canada: New Society Publishers).

Publications on or by our interview partners

- Benge, J., and G. Benge, (2008) *David Bussau: Facing the World Head-On* (Seattle, WA, USA: YWAM Publishing).
- Bussau, D., and R. Mask (2010) *Christian Microenterprise Development: An Introduction* (Eugene, OR, USA: Wipf & Stock Publishers).
- Lovins, A. (2011) *Reinventing Fire: Bold Business Solutions for the New Energy Era* (Vermont, VT, USA: Chelsea Green Publishing Company).
- Lovins, A. (2011) *The Essential Amory Lovins: Selected Writings* (ed. Cameron M. Burns; New York: Routledge).
- Mehta, P.K., and S. Shenoy (2011) *Infinite Vision: How Aravind Became the World's Greatest Business Case for Compassion* (San Francisco, CA, USA: Berrett-Koehler Publishers, Inc.).
- Minney. S. (2011) *Naked Fashion: The New Sustainable Fashion Revolution* (Oxford, UK: New Internationalist Publications Ltd).
- Natural World Museum (2008) *Art in Action: Nature, Creativity, and Our Collective Future* (USA: Mandala Publishing Group).
- Polak, P. (2009) *Out of Poverty: What Works When Traditional Approaches Fail* (San Francisco, CA, USA: Berrett-Koehler Publishers, Inc.).
- Suzuki, D. (2007) *David Suzuki: The Autobiography* (Vancouver, Canada: Greystone Books).
- Suzuki, D. (2007) *The Sacred Balance: Rediscovering Our Place in Nature* (Vancouver, Canada: Greystone Books).
- Suzuki, D. (2004) *The David Suzuki Reader: A Lifetime of Ideas from a Leading Activist and Thinker* (Vancouver, Canada: Greystone Books).
- Suzuki, D., and M. Atwood (Foreword) (2011) *The Legacy: An Elder's Vision for Our Sustainable Future* (Vancouver, Canada: Greystone Books).
- Suzuki, D., and I. Hanington (2012) *Everything under the Sun: Toward a Brighter Future on a Small Blue Planet* (Vancouver, Canada: Greystone Books).

- Tyndale, P. (2004) *Don't Look Back: The David Bussau Story: How an Abandoned Child Became a Champion of the Poor* (Crows Nest, NSW, Australia: Allen & Unwin).
- Wood, J. (2006 and 2011) *Leaving Microsoft to Change the World: An Entrepreneur's Odyssey to Educate the World's Children* (New York: Collins).

APPENDIX 4
Photo credits

Aravind Augenklinik:
Pages 51, 114

Arboleda, Clarita:
Page 122 bottom of page

Büro Prof. Muhammad Yunus:
Page 219

Bussau, David:
Page 111 top of page

Caamaño, Cristina:
Page 81

Collopy, Michael/Skoll Foundation:
Pages 57

Crear Vale la Pena:
Page 119

Escuela Nueva:
Page 94 top of page

Eyre, Chris:
Page 116 bottom of page

Ganju, Erin:
Page 151

Grupo Nueva:
Page 39

Khosla, Ashok:
Page 143

Krämer, Florian:
Page 87

Laster, Diane:
Page 120 bottom of page

Legacy Ventures:
Page 33

Maas, John-Michael/Darby Communications:
Pages 118, 157

Natural World Museum:
Pages 73, 120 top of page

People Tree:
Page 25, 111 bottom of page

Rocky Mountains Institute/Judy Hill:
Page 179

Room to Read:
Page 123

Skoll Foundation:
Pages 101, 113 top of page, 115, 116 top of page

Stefańska Hafenmayer, Joanna:
Pages 19, 95, 109, 110, 112, 117, 121, 127, 135, 167, 173, 187, 193, 199

Stefańska Hafenmayer, Joanna/ Hafenmayer, Wolfgang:
Pages 2, 124

Stop:
Page 113 bottom of page